Sensory Stimulation

Sensory Stimulation

Sensory-Focused Activities for People with Physical and Multiple Disabilities

Susan Fowler

Foreword by Hilary Johnson, Manager, Communication Resource Centre, Scope (Vic.) Ltd

Jessica Kingsley Publishers
London and Philadelphia

First published in 1997
by Coa Press, a division of the Spastic Society of Victoria

This edition published in 2007
by Jessica Kingsley Publishers
116 Pentonville Road
London N1 9JB, UK
and
400 Market Street, Suite 400
Philadelphia, PA 19106, USA

www.jkp.com

Library of Congress Cataloging in Publication Data
Fowler, Susan, 1960-
  Sensory stimulation : sensory-focused activities for people with physical and multiple disabilities / Susan Fowler ; published with Scope (Vic) Ltd ; foreword by Hilary Johnson.
     p. ; cm.
  Originally pub.: Sensory stimulation theory and activities for adults with physical and multiple disabilites. Melbourne : Spastic Society of Victoria, 1997.
  Includes bibliographical references.
  ISBN-13: 978-1-84310-455-1 (pbk.)
  ISBN-10: 1-84310-455-5 (pbk.)
  1. Arts--Therapeutic use. 2. Disabled--Rehabilitation. 3. Perceptual-motor learning. 4. Active learning. 5. Sensory stimulation. I. Fowler, Susan, 1960- Sensory stimulation theory and activities for adults with physical and multiple disabilites. II. Scope (Victoria) III. Title.
  [DNLM: 1. Sensory Art Therapies--methods. 2. Disabled Persons--rehabilitation. 3. Education, Special--methods. WB 555 F788s 2006]
  RC489.A72F692 2006
  616.89'1656--dc22
                             2006020804

British Library Cataloguing in Publication Data
A CIP catalogue record for this book is available from the British Library

ISBN-13: 978 1 84310 455 1
ISBN-10: 1 84310 455 5

Printed and bound in Great Britain by
Printwise (Haverhill) Ltd, Suffolk

This book includes a resource of ideas for sensory-focused activities. Some of the activities and recipes described in this book may not be appropriate for some individuals. It is the responsibility of the user to ensure that any activity or recipe is selected and/or modified with due consideration given to the individual needs and abilities of each participant. The author can not be held responsible for any negative consequences resulting from the use of activities in this book.

Contents

APPENDICES

LIST OF ACTIVITIES

Personal and household care

Art and craft

Foreword

Our senses play an integral role in developing our personalities, skills and knowledge. People who have limited communication often have decreased opportunities to develop their use of touch, taste, smell, sound and sight. We sometimes refer to people with little or no speech as having complex communication needs. An inability to communicate formally by speech, pictures or writing often leads to communication partners restricting their social interaction. This becomes a limiting cycle where the staff and carers do not know how to communicate effectively and so less and less communication occurs. A book like this one assists anyone who interacts with someone with complex communication needs.

People who are unable to communicate through speech, pictures, signs or spelling may have a range of disabling conditions. These might include intellectual or cognitive disabilities, learning disabilities, severe physical limitations, complex health needs and/or severe epilepsy. No disability should result in people being excluded from the community as we all benefit from being included and participating with others around fun activities. Even now when approaches such as person-centred planning and individual plans are used, some people with disabilities spend much of the day in congregate care activities that are poorly funded and where interaction time is at a premium. This is where this resource becomes very powerful. It not only offers a framework to understand why you might do an activity; it also provides a range of different ideas, which require a minimum of setting-up time. These activities promote the individuality of each person involved, allowing for the emergence or development of preference.

The material in this resource arose through work with support staff in both day and residential services, though it has been written in such a way that it can be used by a range of relevant professionals. The assessment tools are practical and easy to apply. The activities incorporate a wide range of sensory activities utilising theoretically sound principles in working with people with severe and profound disabilities. The structure of the activities is consistent, giving readers with creative ideas a template to further develop their own activities. This book is an excellent practical resource and will be a great 'cookbook' for many workers in the field.

Hilary Johnson
Manager, Communication Resource Centre
Scope (Vic.) Ltd

Acknowledgements

I would like to express my thanks to friends and colleagues for their contribution of activity ideas and support during the writing of this book. In particular, I would like to thank Mandy Williams, Hilary Johnson, Terry Martin, Robyn Collins, Lee Darling, Sheridan Foster, Mark Demarco and Nick Hagiliassis for their advice and input. I would like to thank Darren Blenkinsop for the drawings. Thanks must also go to Ralda Bourne, who not only organised the funding and printing of this book, but gave me the impetus to finish it. Her time, advice, input, support and organisational skills have been invaluable.

My thanks go, too, to the following people and organisations, who have kindly contributed activities: Judith Arthur, support worker, Scope (Victoria), Australia (Grapefruit sorbet, p.124); Rita Attard, support worker, Scope (Victoria), Australia (Rita's sponge finger cake, p.136); my friend, Cally Bennett (Soy banana thick milkshake, p.103); Leanne Crawford, sensory art consultant, Victoria, Australia (Cinnamon clay ornaments, p.178, Cinnamon spice dough, p.179, Warm cornflour finger paint, p.196, Foil painting/corrugated card, p.183, Glitter leisure dough, p.184, Soapy paint, p.195, Yoghurt painting, p.198), and with Suzannah Burton, therapy aide, Scope (Victoria), Australia (Christmas tree cards, p.176); Andrea Dalli, Michael Burns and Lisa Reid, support workers, Scope (Victoria), Australia (Hand lotion, p.151); my neighbour, Eileen Darling (Wool mix, p.169) my mother, Mary Fowler (Avocado dip, p.111); Wendy Fowler, support worker, St Nicholas House, Oxford, UK (Icing sugar art, p.188); Heather Inglis, occupational therapist, Australia (Refreshing peppermint foot cream, p.159); Debbie Joy, occupational therapist (Fluorescent action painting, p.181); Helen McLinden, support worker, Scope (Victoria), Australia (Kosciusko nightcap, p.94, Fruit cheese roll, p.121); Claire McNamara and Bev Graham, support workers, Scope (Victoria), Australia (Bath salts, p.149); Scope Outworks Day Services (Victoria), Australia (Sweet violet hand cream, p.168); my friend, Heather Tumber (Summer pudding, p.142); Veanne Wills Nepean School, Victoria, Australia (Peppermint face mask, p.157, Rich yoghurt and fruit exfoliating mask, p.161).

Finally, I would like to thank my husband, Adrian Bone, for the support and advice he has given me. I also thank him for his patience while I have been engrossed in finishing this book.

While every care has been taken to trace and acknowledge copyright, the author tenders apologies for any accidental infringement where ownership has proved untraceable.

Introduction

Over the years, sensory stimulation programmes have been provided for people with physical and multiple disabilities. Multisensory rooms, also known as 'snoezelen™' rooms, have also been developed to provide sensory-stimulating environments for people to explore. However, those working with people with profound and multiple disabilities are often not sure *why* they are providing sensory-focused activities, what activities to provide and what to do in the multisensory rooms.

In this resource, the term 'sensory programme' has been replaced with 'sensory-focused activity'. This is to shift the focus away from providing sensory programmes per se, and to encourage people to look at *all* activities within a person's life and present them in a sensory-focused way. The intention is to enable people to participate in these activities, which have meaning for them.

In recent times there has been a move to provide sensory environments that match a person's sensory threshold – that is, the amount of sensory input they can process and cope with (Dunn 1999a, 1999b). Whether or not a person needs more or less sensory input in their environment, the activities presented in this resource can still be used. They are set out in a structured way, using sensory cues. Thus, those who need more sensory input will get the extra sensory cues they need to work out what is going on in their environment. For those who get overstimulated easily, the cues and predictability help them anticipate what is about to happen and thus reduce their anxiety.

This resource looks at some everyday activities, such as making drinks and meals, beauty care and using household products, as well as art and craft. The activities described are provided primarily for enjoyment and leisure, as well as giving everyone the opportunity to participate in them. They are not based on sensory integration therapy; however, they can be used to provide controlled sensory input to elicit an adaptive response, in an attempt to replace non-purposeful self-engagement behaviours. They also incorporate a learning component as people may develop skills whilst carrying out sensory-focused activities (e.g. switching skills), which improve their ability to participate more fully in activities they enjoy.

Part One explores some theories that give a framework for providing sensory-focused activities, and clarifies why sensory-focused activities are provided. It considers assessments and sets out some ideas on how to structure sensory-focused activities in order to maximise participation. It also describes an example of a programme that was developed to teach support people how to run sensory-focused activities.

Part Two sets out some sensory-focused activities. It takes everyday activities and recipes and shows how these can be presented in a sensory-stimulating way, by emphasising the process and not just the end product.

Included at the beginning of Part Two is an outline for presenting everyday activities so that they have a sensory focus and maximise a person's participation in that activity. There are also template sheets that can be copied and used to help plan sensory-focused activities, as well as examples of recording forms.

The activities have been divided into four sections: drinks, food, personal and household care, and art and craft. The activities chosen use everyday equipment, the ingredients are readily available and they can easily be incorporated into day-to-day life.

This book is primarily written for people supporting those with physical and multiple disabilities and is fully photocopiable so the information, activities and form templates can be passed around, and used again and again. The resource also has 'lay-flat binding', which allows the material to be copied with ease.

PART ONE

THEORY

1

The Meaning of Sensory Stimulation

Every day we receive information from our senses: when we walk down the street, visit the market, eat a meal, when we get up in the morning and wash and dress. We learn about our world through our senses, and by interacting with our environment. Children explore and play, and in doing so they learn about their surroundings; for example, they find out what things hurt them or burn them, what things are fragile and need to be handled delicately, what things can be eaten and what can be played with. This process of exploration continues throughout our lives. We constantly explore and examine new things – moving, smelling, tasting, feeling, looking and listening – and thus discover their various properties. From this we can make decisions on whether or not we like the new object or experience.

As a result of physical, sensory or intellectual disabilities, and/or living in non-stimulating surroundings, many people with disabilities have not had the same opportunity to explore and interact with their environment. The impact of an impoverished environment has also been studied in relation to children who lived in orphanages in eastern Europe (Cermak and Daunhaur 1997; Lin *et al.* 2005). The studies highlighted the 'critical importance of the environment for sensory integration' (Cermak and Daunhaur 1997, p.500) and many of the children were observed to be 'almost completely silent, engaging in self stimulating behaviours such as rocking, scratching or staring at their fingers' (Cermak and Daunhaur 1997, p.500).

One of the aims of providing sensory-focused activities is to provide environments in which people can have the opportunity to use their various senses: to move, touch, smell, taste, hear and see. People with disabilities need to be supported to help them make use of their senses and to interact with their environment, thus assisting them to learn about their world. This may be through interacting with their social environment, with other people, or their physical environment where they are directly involved in smelling, tasting, reaching for objects, and so on.

The aim of providing sensory-focused activities is to activate or stimulate the sensory system. The effects of stimulating the sensory system can either be excitatory or inhibitory. Some types of sensory stimulation will make the person more alert and attentive, while others (e.g. massage) will have a relaxing effect.

Sensory-focused activities are not the same as sensory stimulation programmes that are carried out once a week, but instead are incorporated into everyday life. Sensory experiences can be found in many activities – for example, assisting people to feel/smell toiletries, putting scented oils in the bath, putting lavender bags in the wardrobe or offering people different types of tea and coffee. When outside, assist people to feel the grass, crush dry leaves, feel the bark of trees and smell flowers.

Getting around in the local community can also be a sensory experience – visiting a perfume counter, for instance, or a market, which is full of different noises, smells and textures. Be prepared to observe carefully as someone with a disability may have only very small reactions to many different stimuli (e.g. do they move their heads to feel the wind on their faces, do they become still when listening to the sounds about them, or do they look at the bright lights in the shopping centre?). However, be aware that some environments, such as the market, may be overstimulating for some. With creative thinking, many ordinary daily activities can be presented with a sensory focus.

2

Theoretical Framework for Sensory-Focused Activities

The purpose of this chapter is to provide an overview of some of the main conceptual models that have guided how and why sensory activities are selected. A number of theories have been drawn on; however, this section is not intended to provide an exhaustive review of all literature in this field. If you wish to read more around the subject refer to the Further reading section, which follows the References.

The following frameworks are used when considering how to provide activities that have meaning for people and that encourage participation. This is in terms of:

- working out which sensory system people most prefer to use and whether they prefer to engage with objects or people (engagement behaviours)

- the intensity of sensory input they prefer (sensory threshold)

- the level of understanding

- the level of communication (communication before speech/Triple C (Checklist of Communication Competencies), see p.24)

- how to encourage communication (intensive interaction)

- the importance of providing sensory environments (snoezelen™)

- the importance of valuing people (person-centred thinking) and providing inclusive activities.

These frameworks should be used as guiding principles for selecting and conducting activities.

The Individualised Sensory Environment (ISE)
Engagement questionnaire (Karen Bunning 1991–1993)

Karen Bunning is a research speech language therapist who developed the concept of the Individualised Sensory Environment (ISE) for people with severe learning difficulties. 'The ISE aims to increase the purposeful, adaptive responses of the people and to decrease the levels of self engagement behaviour' (Bunning 1996). As part of her work Bunning devised an engagement background questionnaire that looks at self-engagement, object engagement and person–object engagement (see Appendix 1). Although she was unable to prove the questionnaire's reliability, it is still a useful tool for establishing baseline engagement behaviours.

Completing the questionnaire highlights the types of engagement behaviours exhibited. The questionnaire needs to be filled out by someone who knows the person with a disability well. The self-engagement section of the questionnaire is used as a baseline behaviour (for a definition of baseline see Chapter 4, p.39). The aim is to present people with different sensory environments to see whether or not the self-engagement behaviours decrease or stop. This is based on two premises:

1. that the self-engagement behaviours are due to a lack of stimulation. For people who have been understimulated for many years these behaviours may now have become part of their usual routine; however, if they are provided with objects or activities that capture their attention they may still reduce their self-engagement behaviours

2. that the self-engagement behaviours indicate that a person is overstimulated and using the sensory system they feel safest with to either block out or distract them from the overwhelming sensations coming from their environment.

Careful observations of the environment and the mood of the person help determine whether they are exhibiting self-engagement behaviours to give themselves more sensory input or to calm themselves. For example, are they happy and relaxed when showing self-engagement behaviours, or are they anxious and overwhelmed? Taking a sensory history can also help work out whether or not a person is under- or overstimulated (see the following section, on the sensory profile).

The person and object parts of the engagement background questionnaire show whether or not a person is interacting with the people and objects. To be functional, he or she must interact with both. For example, if a person is learning to eat independently, he or she has to interact with the object, the spoon, to pick it up, hold it and take it to his or her mouth. He or she also needs to interact with other people and acknowledge their presence in order to listen to instructions and respond to praise when they succeed at the task.

Often people with profound and multiple disabilities exhibit many self-engagement behaviours but few person or object engagement behaviours. The aim is to move them away from these self-engagement behaviours and on to engaging with people and objects.

The sensory profile

The Infant Toddler Sensory Profile (Dunn 2002), *The Adult Sensory Profile* (Brown and Dunn 2002) and *The Sensory Profile Manual* (Dunn 1999b) are three manuals that between them cover the sensory profiles of people from birth to the age of 90 and above. Sensory profile measures are questionnaires about how people respond to sensory experiences in everyday life. The three manuals (or 'tools') cover the entire life span; the children's versions are completed by parents/caregivers, and the adolescent/adult version is completed by the individual her- or himself. A fourth measure, the School Companion Sensory Profile, asks teachers to complete questions on selected students (see www.sensoryprofile.com for more detailed information, including technical reports, frequently asked questions and a bibliography).

The sensory profile looks at people's *sensory thresholds* and their *behavioural responses* to those thresholds. It is important to have an understanding of these concepts as knowing about 'sensory processing is empowering as sensory processing preferences can explain an individual's response to particular environments, situations, activities and people' (Brown 2001, p.117).

Thresholds are the point at which nerves are activated by the sensations they receive. 'A low threshold indicates that the nervous system requires less stimuli for an individual to recognise a sensation. Conversely, a high threshold requires more intense sensory stimulation for the neuron to fire and for the individual to recognize the sensation' (Brown 2001, p.117). We all have different thresholds – for example, pain thresholds, where some people can tolerate more pain than others. Our thresholds also fluctuate in that sometimes we can cope with more pain than at other times. This applies to our other senses as well (e.g. movement, touch, vision, hearing, taste and smell).

The sensory profile analyses answers to specific questions about how people respond to sensory events in their everyday life. From this it can be worked out whether a person has a high or low sensory threshold. People with *high* sensory thresholds *need more sensory input* in their life than they get from their everyday activities. Those with *low* sensory thresholds *need less sensory input* than they get from everyday activities and consequently are often *overstimulated*.

Not only do people have different sensory thresholds, but they can also react differently to them. They can accept their thresholds and be passive about them. Alternatively, they can do something active in order to meet those thresholds.

The combination of sensory thresholds and behavioural responses to those thresholds gives four descriptors of behaviour (Dunn 2001):

1. *High* sensory threshold, *passive* behavioural response – Low registration (needs more sensory input, i.e. is not registering cues from self or the environment).

2. *High* sensory threshold, *active* behavioural response – Sensory seeking (creates more sensory input and enjoys input).

3. *Low* sensory threshold, *passive* behavioural response – Sensory sensitivity (needs less sensory input).

4. *Low* sensory threshold, *active* behavioural response – Sensory avoiding (withdraws from sensory input).

Many people use the adult/adolescent profile with adults with disabilities. However, because caregivers rather than the people themselves answer the questions, the results from the profile can be used only as an indication of a person's sensory threshold. This information is then used in conjunction with observations and interviews with people who know the person well.

The learning continuum (Barbara Knickerbocker 1980); a holistic sensory approach (Helen Sanderson and Niki Gitsham 1991)

Barbara Knickerbocker's work provides a cognitive framework (i.e. what a person is understanding in terms of a five-stage learning continuum). This has been expanded on by Helen Sanderson and Niki Gitsham, who applied these stages to people with profound learning disabilities. The five stages are described below.

I. AVOID

This is thought to be the first stage of learning for people with physical and multiple disabilities. In this stage, people either avoid stimuli by being very passive, pulling away from touching things, physically removing themselves from the group or curling up in a corner. They may also be so hyperactive that they never spend long enough in one place to take notice of the stimuli around them. The aim at this stage is to assist the person to make contact with their surroundings, to know that things exist outside themselves.

If people are at the Avoid stage, begin with non-touch activities as they will find touch irritating or threatening. For example, use bubbles, smells, sounds, wind and suchlike to gain people's attention and to build up trust before attempting to touch them. The next step is to work towards indirect stimulation that does not require touch (e.g. massage using different-textured mitts). When massaging this group of people use firm pressure. Light touch can be experienced as irritating and uncomfortable, causing the person to pull away or become agitated. Consult with a physiotherapist or masseur for instructions on how to handle and massage people appropriately. In addition, consult with an occupational therapist to set up specific programmes for individuals who cannot tolerate touch.

At the Avoid level, items are presented to people to assist them to explore rather than the individuals actively exploring their environment and objects. They need to feel safe and non-threatened within their environment. It is a time to build up trust so, if someone pulls away, let them and if they want to wander off allow them to go, although continue to provide supervision if required. When someone wants to leave a room, it may be that they are overstimulated and this is their way of reducing the sensory input to a level they can tolerate. Facilitate people to feel that they have some control over the situation.

During this Avoid stage, some people may also exhibit self-engagement behaviours (e.g. finger flicking or rocking). This may be their way of shutting out sensory input as the environment is overstimulating. However, people may also exhibit self-engagement behaviours to give themselves sensory input. They have not yet discovered that they can gain sensory input from their environment and so are inwardly focused, using their bodies to provide sensory input. It is important that those supporting people with profound and multiple disabilities know them well and are observant of their moods – are they happy and relaxed when showing self-engagement behaviours, or are they anxious and overwhelmed?

Whatever the reason for people exhibiting self-engagement behaviours, they will use the sensory system they are most motivated by or comfortable with. Use of self-engagement behaviours suggests that there may initially have been some understanding of cause and effect in relation to themselves (e.g. 'I know that when I rock it feels good'). However, there may no longer be any conscious thought about why they use these behaviours; they have just become a routine.

2. EXPLORE

In this stage people begin to actively explore their surroundings, objects and other people, and to develop preferences. During the course of their exploration they may make a movement that produces an unexpected result that they like and they will later repeat that movement. People with profound and multiple disabilities may initially need help to explore, and their unintentional behaviours may need to be moulded. Thus, if a person is interested in a light, a lamp could be linked up with a switch. The switch could be placed in front of the person, who is co-actively assisted to operate it and get the reward of the light coming on. At first, they may not realise that they are operating the switch but if this behaviour is constantly reinforced they may in time learn the concept of cause and effect.

People who exhibit sensory defensiveness may not initially tolerate touch for co-active assistance. They may reach out and touch things, but the experiences must be within their control. However, if a person's trust is gained, and they know that they can stop at any time, they may tolerate co-active assistance. For people who cannot tolerate touch, set up the piece of equipment that motivates them, and position it nearby to enable them to accidentally activate it. In some circumstances an external switch may be required to achieve this. Thus, in the course of their normal movements, they may touch the equipment/switch and begin to develop an understanding of cause and effect: 'When I press the switch, the light comes on, but I'm not sure how I did it.'

3. ORGANISE

At this stage, people have learnt cause and effect and the concept of object permanence (i.e. an understanding that something still exists even if they cannot see it). Thus, if a cloth were placed over a switch, they would know that the switch was still there and move the cloth off the switch to enable them to use it.

This is also the stage at which people discriminate between different stimuli. For example, they know if objects are similar (e.g. the rug and scarf are soft) and also know that objects are different (e.g. the rug is soft and the floor is hard).

4. INTEGRATE

During this stage, people begin to use all their senses together to explore their surroundings and to develop an understanding of different aspects of their environment. They are able to integrate experiences with the present (e.g. 'I felt that before and liked it'). They will begin to experiment: if they know that banging a drum will produce a sound they may bang a light switch to see if they will also get a sound from this. Alternatively, they may find that the 'same object will do different things' or make different noises 'depending on how it is used' (Sanderson and Gitsham 1991). From a functional point of view, when people are at this stage and can press a switch for one object (e.g. to turn on a light) they could also be taught that pressing other switches can turn on other objects (e.g. a cassette recorder or food processor). Remember, however, that it is often the case that people with disabilities can not generalise skills, so will need to be taught to operate different pieces of equipment in different environments.

5. CONCEPTUALISE

By this stage, people are no longer using trial and error. They are able to problem-solve by thinking about things, and their behaviour is intentional.

Framework for recognising attainment (Claire Marvin 1998)

This is another framework developed in the UK. It is used by teachers to help them recognise attainment below Level 1 of the National Curriculum. However, the framework can also be applied to people with profound and multiple disabilities engaging in everyday activities. It offers a useful way to describe how much people are interacting with their environment.

The framework looks at changes in responses and behaviour as people become more involved in a learning process or activity. For example, someone may be present during an activity, but not actively engaged (known as Encounter, see below) or they can generalise the skills they have learnt and participate actively in a number of activities (Gaining Skills).

However, it must be kept in mind that people will not necessarily move through all the stages in a sequential way. Their responses can change from day to day and also depending on the context or activity being presented. In this instance, it could indicate a greater interest in one activity over another.

ENCOUNTER

People are present during the experience or activity but are not participating in it. They may therefore experience different sensory inputs (e.g. hot/cold). For some, however, the fact that they will stay in a room and be present is an achievement in itself.

AWARENESS

People appear to show awareness that something has happened. They show fleeting awareness of an object, event or person (e.g. briefly stop their self-engagement behaviours or are startled by the sound of a door slamming).

ATTENTION AND RESPONSE

People attend and begin to respond, although inconsistently. For example, they show signs of surprise, enjoyment or frustration. They also demonstrate the beginnings of the ability to distinguish between different people, objects, events and places.

ENGAGEMENT

People pay more consistent attention to events. They can tell the difference between specific events in their surroundings. For example, they may focus their looking or listening, turn to locate people, objects or events, or follow moving objects. When people are demonstrating consistent responses to stimuli, it is possible to compile lists of their likes and dislikes.

PARTICIPATION

People engage with others, sharing and turn-taking. They anticipate familiar sequences of events. They react rather than reaching out to actively explore their environment. Explorations of objects or interactions with people are initiated by others.

INVOLVEMENT

People actively reach out to objects or people. This is not just a passive exploration of what is put in front of people – they are more proactive, reaching out to objects or people.

GAINING SKILLS

People gain, strengthen or make general use of their skills. For example, they may communicate that they prefer different activities/environments.

Firth (2004) has adapted this framework for recognising attainment as a recording system for use when assessing attainment during intensive interaction (see below). Thus, instead of using it for interaction with the general environment, it is specific to social interactions. There are still seven levels but the final level has been changed from Gaining Skills to Student Initiated Interaction. During this stage the person 'Independently starts an activity (that cannot be described as repetitive or self absorbed behaviour) and engages another person in the activity with social intent' (Firth 2004, p.3).

The Affective Communicating Assessment (ACA) (Judith Coupe O'Kane and Juliet Goldbart 1998); The Triple C – Checklist of Communication Competencies (Karen Bloomberg and Denise West 1999)

Judith Coupe O'Kane and Juliet Goldbart have identified six levels at which people communicate, including three levels of pre-intentional and three levels of intentional communication.

Karen Bloomberg and Denise West have developed the Triple C – Checklist of Communication Competencies, based on Coupe O'Kane and Goldbart's work. It is a communication assessment designed for use with adolescents and adults who have severe or multiple disabilities. It provides a checklist of abilities that are grouped together to form communication stages.

In general, people with profound and multiple disabilities communicate at either an unintentional or informal intentional level. These four levels are outlined below.

LEVEL 1 – REFLEXIVE

At this stage, people's responses are reflexive but others will assign meaning and communicative intent to these behaviours. At this level, people appear to sleep a lot and will look only at others or objects that come into their field of vision. People are internally focused and need to be encouraged to interact with the external world. At this stage a person may be watching, but not reacting to, objects or people.

LEVEL 2 – REACTIVE

At this stage, people will react to different stimuli and their behaviours are assigned meaning (e.g. like/dislike). They are at the Explore stage of the learning continuum. They will be able to differentiate between different tones of voice, facial expression and body language, and react accordingly. At this level people will not initiate interaction, but will react to it. They can, however, respond to consistent routines.

LEVEL 3 – PROACTIVE

At this level, people will reach out to explore their environment. They are beginning to show some person and object interaction and can recognise some objects that have meaning for them (e.g. cup means drink). They are still at the Explore level on the learning continuum, where they may make a movement that produces an unexpected result that they like and they will, therefore, repeat that movement later. When interacting with objects, people will use them in different ways such as shaking them, banging them against a table or another object, or throwing them to the floor. By the time they understand cause and effect their communication has become intentional, because they know that when they do something they will get a response.

LEVEL 4 – INTENTIONAL INFORMAL

At this level people begin to communicate intentionally, using objects and people to get their message across. They recognise familiar people and use some gestures, such as pointing. They will also use people to achieve what they want (e.g. putting a caregiver's hand on a spoon to indicate that they want another mouthful of food). They understand some simple commands, such as 'sit down' or 'give me', but these need to be in context.

People also engage with objects and will use them to gain another person's attention. They will use a variety of actions on an object. This stage corresponds with the Organise stage of the learning continuum.

Bloomberg and West are looking at changing the terminology and also combining the Reflexive and Reactive stages. The reasons they give for combining the first two levels are that there are very few adults who are at the Reflexive level and the intervention for both levels is the same – that is, 'looking at quality of life, sensory activities and developing awareness in the communication partner's skills' (Personal communication 2005).

The new levels proposed are:

- Stage 1: unintentional passive (previously reflexive and reactive)
- Stage 2: unintentional active (previously proactive)
- Stage 3: intentional informal (as before).

Intensive interaction (Melanie Nind and David Hewett 2001)

Intensive interaction describes a way of communicating with people with profound and multiple disabilities. It is suited to people who may be withdrawn in their communication and who have very few social communication skills. It is based on the interaction style that a parent has with a young baby and the focus is on the process of interaction rather than its outcome. Thus, the aim is to spend time together and interact with each other in such a way that the person feels safe and engaged. It is not about the exchange of information or getting a specific need met but rather aims to demonstrate to the person that they are good to spend time with. This is also described by Kennedy (2001).

A central idea of intensive interaction is using the language that the person with a disability uses. They may make sounds to themselves, tap or rub objects, or make idiosyncratic movements. The interaction partner can use this language to engage with them. They may respectfully mime the person's sounds or reflect certain movements. This often captures the attention of the person with a disability, as the behaviours that they are seeing in their interaction partner are familiar to them.

PRINCIPLES OF INTENSIVE INTERACTION

- Be aware of where the person feels most comfortable and use this as a place for interactions.

- Slow down and take time.

- Build in pauses so that people can take turns with actions, movements and sounds.

- Relax – think about body language and be present in mind and body (people can sense if they are not getting full attention).

- Share the control of the interaction, sometimes leading and sometimes following.

- Create and repeat familiar, mutually enjoyable routines.

Respond to:

- vocalisations

- other noises made with the mouth

- other noises

- movements

- facial expression

- physical contact

- stereotypical behaviour.

Respond by:

- imitating

- joining in

- saying something

- being dramatic

- using non-speech sounds

- providing a running commentary (although be aware that this could be overstimulating for some people).

The 'snoezelen™' concept (Jan Hulsegge and Ad Verheul 1987)

People with profound and multiple disabilities often operate on a sensory level. Developmentally, they are more interested in exploring the sensations they get from their bodies and environment, rather than trying to understand complex concepts. This is the basis of the snoezelen™ philosophy.

Snoezelen™ is a concept that was developed in the Netherlands by Hulsegge and Verheul (1987). The term is a contraction of two Dutch words meaning 'sniffing' and 'dozing' and is meant to convey the feeling of activity or exploration (as in sniffing) combined with relaxation (dozing). Originally it was a very nebulous concept and was applied to any activity that stimulated the senses in an attractive environment.

Although Hulsegge and Verheul talked about 'snoezelen™' rooms, they viewed the concept in a much broader sense. Snoezelen™ is more the activity of enjoying a sensory-stimulating environment, rather than the room itself. Taking this definition, snoezelen™ can occur when having a shower, cooking a meal, being in the park, lying on the beach or sitting by the fire enjoying a glass of wine. The main point is that a person is enjoying the sensory aspects of the activity. Unfortunately, some people have restricted multisensory work to specific rooms, rather than seeing that all activities can be presented in a sensory way.

The fundamentals of the snoezelen™ philosophy include:

- creating an atmosphere of trust and relaxation

- providing a pleasant atmosphere that appeals to the senses

- presenting everyday activities with a sensory focus

- permitting the person with a disability to set the pace

- giving people choices

- emphasising the importance of support partners' attitudes – giving people time and space to explore

- stressing the importance of physical contact and building a relationship with people.

Under the snoezelen™ concept, the aim is for people to explore their surroundings without feeling the need to achieve anything. They taste, smell, touch, move 'because they like it, not to acquire information or to learn from it or develop' (Hulsegge and Verheul 1987).

Joe Kewin sums up snoezelen™ in the following way: 'The essence of "snoezelen" is to allow the individual the time, space and opportunity to enjoy the environment at their own pace, free from the expectations of others' (in Hutchinson 1991, p.9).

Snoezelen™ is therefore regarded 'primarily as a form of relaxation' (Hulsegge and Verheul 1987). However, the authors also state that skill development may be a spin-off from snoezelen™ rooms, although they 'do not wish to give development and therapy a central function within "snoezelen"' (Hulsegge and Verheul 1987).

Person-centred planning (Helen Sanderson 2000); Philosophy of the five service accomplishments (John O'Brien 1989)

'Person centred planning is based on new ways of seeing and working with people with disabilities, fundamentally about sharing power and community inclusion' (Sanderson 2000, p.1). It puts the person in the centre of the planning process when providing services, rather than providing services and fitting the person into a service that may not meet their individual needs. It has been influenced by the philosophy of the 'five service accomplishments' (see below), and by normalisation and social role valorisation, which looks at helping people to achieve accepted roles in the community and to have a good quality of life.

People with profound and multiple disabilities are unable to verbalise what they like and dislike, and this has implications for providing a quality service and activities that they really enjoy.

The above frameworks provide important information to be used during person-centred planning. For example, people with profound and multiple disabilities operate at a sensory level, so it is important to provide meaningful sensory environments and activities. They are unable to say what they like or dislike, but are able to indicate, through their behaviour, what they like in terms of sensory systems and sensory thresholds. By understanding how a person communicates and the level at which they communicate and understand, activities can be provided that have meaning to that person. The implementation of intensive interaction practices ensures that the person is valued, as their individual styles of communication are recognised and support people make a commitment to learn these styles of interaction. There is also a commitment to spending time just enjoying being with and interacting with the person with a disability.

The following section outlines the five service accomplishments (O'Brien 1989) that are the elements of quality service delivery for people with profound and multiple disabilities. These elements are described below with some discussion as to how each relates to sensory-focused activities.

RESPECT

O'Brien (1989) emphasised that people should be respected at all times and that other people's attitudes are important when interacting with people who have a disability. It is how that interaction takes place that demonstrates respect for another person. This means that support people should take the time to see what people like and when they have had enough or want a change. They also need to be aware of the external environment and change it if it is too noisy and over-stimulating.

The role of support people is one of facilitation so that people with a disability can become as independent as possible, exercising choice and controlling aspects of their sensory environment. Support people should also focus on encouraging valued social roles, whereby people experience 'the dignity and status associated with positively regarded activities' (O'Brien and Lyle 1987, p.21).

CHOICE

People with profound and multiple disabilities are often perceived as not being capable of making choices. However, most people are able to make choices even if they are unable to verbalise them. Time needs to be spent with them, working out how they make choices, by observing their behaviours; these will indicate whether or not they like or dislike certain food, clothing or activities.

People can be offered choices about whether or not to engage in an activity. They can also make choices about which aspects of an activity they wish to participate in.

CAPABILITIES

Most people have the ability to learn or refine certain skills. It is important to work out what motivates people and use this information to help them develop their skills. This may be as simple as observing a person's reactions to certain things and how they react when they like something. When people's attempts at communicating are responded to they can learn that a certain action or behaviour will bring about a certain response.

During sensory-focused activities, there are many skills that can be taught. These include:

- communication skills, where people are given the opportunity to interact not only with support people but with their peers

- object engagement skills, looking at the different ways people interact with different objects

- cognitive skills such as cause and effect, colour, number and memory.

COMMUNITY PRESENCE

People with profound and multiple disabilities usually live and work in segregated settings. With creative thinking, sensory activities within the wider community can be found that have meaning for people with profound multiple disabilities. For example, there are herb gardens to visit, listening posts in music shops, perfume counters at department stores and different textures to feel at hardware stores and haberdashery shops. A useful activity to carry out is to write down all the different things that can be experienced in the wider community, and list them under the different senses. This ensures that people's sensory preferences can be taken into consideration rather than places being chosen just because they are perceived as sensorily stimulating.

RELATIONSHIPS

Often people with profound and multiple disabilities have restricted social networks and their main support networks predominantly include paid support people. Frequently there is no opportunity even to interact with their peers. Part of the reason for this small social network may be due to the limited opportunity to meet new people. It is therefore important to think about ways of building connections within the local community.

Another reason is that people do not always know how to communicate with a person who has complex communication needs. It is important to document how a person communicates and offer people a range of communication opportunities. If the types of objects and activities that a person with complex communication needs likes can be determined, others can feel more confident about interacting with them, as well as give them something to communicate about.

By taking account of people's sensory preferences, sensory thresholds and communication needs, meaningful activities and environments can be provided within O'Brien's five service accomplishments. For example, take the person who loves strong smells and tastes, and in particular enjoys a strong cappuccino (sensory preference). The way you interact with a person demonstrates your respect for them. It is also acknowledged that coffee is very important to this person, so this activity can be developed further (respect). Instead of just having a coffee at the day centre, visit the local coffee shop that is part of that person's local community (community presence). However, keep in mind that this person has a low threshold for noise and doesn't like to be jostled, so pick a time when the coffee shop isn't busy and crowded (sensory threshold). In becoming a 'regular' at the coffee shop, relationships can be built up with the people who work there (relationships). Finally, competencies can be built in terms of learning the communication skills necessary to request a coffee. This can be done either in terms of using a community request card for *intentional communication* (with a picture/object asking for a coffee) or teaching a person with *unintentional communication* to stand at the counter to indicate that they would like a coffee (capabilities).

Bringing the frameworks together

Figure 2.1 shows how the frameworks discussed in this chapter operate together in providing meaningful sensory-focused activities to maximise participation and communication. Overarching everything are O'Brien's five service accomplishments; these include basic human rights and consider quality-of-life issues.

The person is in the middle of the diagram, emphasising their importance. The activities and environments that are provided are presented in ways that are important to that person.

The main aim is to increase a person's engagement with their physical and social environment. This can be achieved by:

- considering a person's mental and physical health, sensory preferences and sensory thresholds

- providing meaningful activities that take account of
  - level of understanding
  - level of communication and how they communicate

- providing activities and equipment to maximise participation in activities

- considering a person's current capabilities

- thinking about what a person is already doing and the environment that surrounds them.

When considering a person's environment or their context also look at daily routines. Build sensory preferences, thresholds and communication into their daily routines. For example, everyone has a wash at some time; this event is a sensory activity – using different soaps and shampoos. However, the event can be made more or less sensorily stimulating by how it is presented; for example, using unscented bath products or including textured cloths to wash with. The activity can be made more meaningful by helping a person to understand and anticipate what is going to happen – for example, by using object symbols (the person feels the wash cloth to let them know they are going to have a bath or shower).

Also consider the jobs that need to be done in that person's environment. For example, if the fish need to be fed and the person is interested in visual stimulation, it can be their job to feed the fish. If the person is physically unable to feed the fish, they can feel and smell the fish food and watch as the food is placed in the tank and the fish rush to the food.

A model of maximizing participation and communication

Offer choices

Build meaningful relationships

Treat with respect

Provide meaningful activities:
- consider level of understanding
- level of communication
- how people communicate

Consider what a person is already doing/the environment that surrounds them:
- personal daily routines
- jobs that need to be done in their surrounding environment, e.g. at home, work, school, day centre
- consider a person's context

Sensory thresholds
More or less sensory input

Mental health and physical health
Consider these as they also have an impact on engagement with the external environment

Increase engagement with the external environment:
- physical environment – provide meaningful activities and environment
- social environment – intensive interaction

Consider how a person will participate in an activity:
- choose appropriate activity
- choose appropriate equipment
- choose appropriate environment

Consider sensory preferences:
- self-engagement behaviours
- observations during activities
- table of likes/dislikes – determine sensory pattern

Build community connections

Consider capabilities:
- enable people to use skills
- build on abilities
- consider adaptive equipment to increase participation, e.g. supportive wheelchair, adapted handles, switches

Figure 2.1 How the frameworks operate together to provide meaningful sensory-focused activities

3

Maximising Participation in Sensory-Focused Activities

Everyday activities can provide sensory experiences; however, they need to be presented in a structured way in order to teach specific skills and encourage participation. This chapter describes the following ways to maximise participation in sensory-focused activities:

- providing preferred activities and using preferred sensory systems
- taking account of people's sensory thresholds
- decreasing self-engagement behaviours
- promoting an awareness of the external environment
- providing opportunities to make choices and have control over the environment
- promoting communication and therefore person engagement behaviours
- teaching cause and effect
- increasing engagement with objects
- teaching person–object engagement
- selecting appropriate equipment and activities
- providing opportunities to practise skills, make choices and have fun
- community inclusion.

Providing preferred activities and using preferred sensory systems

People will be much more motivated to participate in an activity if they like it. Those with physical and multiple disabilities cannot say what they like, but it can be inferred through their behaviour – for example, smiling or reaching out to preferred objects.

Another way to infer what people like is to look at their self-engagement behaviours, work out which sensory system is being stimulated and then provide activities that stimulate the same sensory system. For example, if someone is rocking and giving themselves movement and touch input, they may enjoy bouncing on a trampoline.

Sensory preferences can determine the types of activities and environments a person may enjoy. For example, if a person likes tactile things they could explore edible paints with their hands and paint using their hands during an art activity. They could also visit tactilely stimulating environments such as a farm, go horse riding, explore different textures in parks and gardens, visit a beautician for a facial or have a massage.

Sensory preferences can also be built into activities. For example, if a person likes vibration, she or he could be the one to hold the electric mixer while making a drink, or the food processor while it chops up nuts.

Sensory thresholds

In order for a person to enjoy and participate in activities, the right amount of sensory input needs to be provided. Having an understanding of a person's sensory threshold will ensure that activities will be presented with the right amount of sensory input (i.e. more or less, depending on a person's threshold). It will also determine the types of environment a person might like. For example, if a person has low sensory thresholds and becomes overwhelmed easily, they would not like to go to the market, where they may be jostled by the crowds, it's noisy, there are a lot of different smells and it's visually overstimulating.

Decrease self-stimulating/self-engagement behaviours

Some people with physical and multiple disabilities display a range of self-stimulating or self-engagement behaviours, such as finger flicking, finger sucking and rocking. One explanation for this is that due to a lack of stimulation, either in the environment or through an inability to access the environment, they seek stimulation from themselves. This is not productive and does not help people to learn or interact with their surroundings.

Self-engagement behaviours are highly arousing and easily obtainable. People need to be taught that other forms of stimulation, external to themselves, can be equally rewarding and self-engagement behaviours can be replaced with these. Although some of the behaviours may initially have been a result of self-stimulation, they may since have become habitual.

If people are exhibiting these behaviours because they are anxious and overwhelmed, they will not be interacting and learning from their surroundings. In such instances, the environment needs to be modified to reduce its overwhelming sensory input, so that the people affected in this way can participate in a preferred activity.

Promoting an awareness of the environment

Many people with profound and multiple disabilities are either passive or preoccupied with their self-stimulating behaviours. Giving them the opportunity to explore their environment allows them to become more aware of things outside themselves; in addition, they may discover an object or activity that interests them.

One of the most challenging aspects for support people is to help the people they work with find something that motivates them. If they have been understimulated for a number of years, or others have not responded to their attempts at communication, they may have reached a stage of learned helplessness, where they are no longer motivated to engage with people or their environment.

Sheila Glenn (1987) worked with children with severe multiple disabilities and found that automated equipment 'under their control' was highly motivating – hence the emphasis on switch activities, where people are able to turn on equipment to participate in an activity (e.g. switch on a food processor to mix ingredients for a cake) or make some change in their environment (e.g. switch on a fan/light).

Providing opportunities to make choices and have control over the environment

Through exploration and a variety of sensory experiences, people are able to develop likes and dislikes. This development is a prerequisite to making informed choices. Offering people the opportunity to make choices enables them to move from having a passive role to taking active control over the things happening to them and their environment.

Promoting communication

Communication is an interactive process between two or more people. People with profound and multiple learning disabilities need to be able to interact with other people for communication to take place. Interaction between people is referred to as 'person engagement' and occurs when people give eye contact, watch people, reach out to people, shake hands and vocalise to others. The aim is to set up a communication environment where there are people to communicate with and who understand the person's way of communication. The environment may be set up to encourage people to use their communication to get something or it can offer a way of using intensive interaction techniques, where people just enjoy having a conversation together.

Glenn (1987) talks about the importance of mutually understood social routines, where people can practise having an effect on their environment through interaction with others. Providing the opportunity and time for people to say hello to each other at the beginning of an activity is just as important as doing the activity itself. This can be set up in a structured way so that they can learn this social routine.

For children, early actions on the environment have social consequences (e.g. I babble and Mum comes and talks to me). People need to be taught that they can have an effect on their social environment through their interaction with others. However, for this to take place, support people need to respond to a person's communication attempts in a consistent manner and reinforce appropriate social interaction. The aim is for people to learn that when they interact appropriately with others, people will stay longer and respond to them.

Not only do opportunities for communication need to be provided, but there also needs to be an understanding of what a person is trying to say before meaningful communication can take place. One way to do this is to chart how people are indicating likes/dislikes/more of and so on, and respond to this in a consistent way. Thus, it is important to record how people react to stimuli, taking notice of any small changes in behaviour. These responses can later be assigned meaning (e.g. like/dislike). Over time, a profile of a person can be built up, indicating the types of thing they like and dislike, and how they indicate these preferences.

For communication to take place, people also need something of interest about which to communicate. Thus, if a person is very interested in an object or activity, set up a way that enables them to indicate that they want more of the thing that interests them (e.g. using an object symbol or looking towards the massage oil to indicate that they want a massage).

Teaching cause and effect with objects

During the development of communication skills, people learn the concept of cause and effect in relation to their social environment (e.g. I smile and vocalise and someone comes and talks to me). In order to gain more control, people also need to be taught cause and effect in relation to their physical environment.

Once people are interested in an object or activity and are able to express preferences, the aim is to teach them cause and effect with objects. Set up the environment to enable people to learn cause and effect – for example, add an external switch to preferred equipment, if necessary, so people can learn, say, when I press the switch, the light comes on.

Increasing engagement with objects

Some people will already be involved with objects that they use in a repetitive manner (e.g. twirling pieces of string or banging objects against their head).

Such people are not using these objects in a functional way or exploring their sensory properties in order to learn about them. They are using them as part of a self-engagement behaviour, as the object is used in a repetitive, non-productive way. While a person is focused on this self-engagement behaviour, they will not be able to participate in other activities. The aim is to increase engagement with other objects in a functional way and thus learn more about the external environment. Object engagement can include looking at an object, watching it move, holding it, feeling and manipulating it. Through this sort of exploration people can learn about the properties of objects.

Following this exploration the aim is to teach a person to use the object functionally, initially through co-active methods. Co-active assistance or physical support is a method of enabling people to carry out an activity that they could not do alone (e.g. support people hold the person's hand and help them to press a switch or hold a spoon). People are then able to participate in an activity and, at the same time, they experience the movement. Consult with an occupational therapist about how to work co-actively with people, as it is important, for instance, to place an object correctly in the palm of the hand, support the limb and ensure that work surfaces are at the correct height.

Teaching person–object engagement

Once a person is interacting with other people and using objects, the aim is to teach them to interact with another person and object at the same time. This is referred to as person–object engagement. Person–object engagement is essential for communication and functional skill development.

Person–object engagement includes passing an object to another person or looking at an object and then at the person. This is done either to indicate that the person wants that object or wants to share an interest in that object with you. Turn-taking opportunities can then be introduced – for example, taking it in turns to use an object or pass a ball back and forth. Turn-taking is a basic skill that is required for communication.

Selecting appropriate equipment and activities

When selecting sensory-focused activities, keep in mind how a person will participate. There is no point choosing to do Christmas cards if these will require a person to stick on small stars or cut out complicated shapes. Think about different ways that the person can be involved – for example, encouraging them to paint using yoghurt paint (see p.198) that has been tinted with Christmas colours and scented with food essences. Someone else may be able to cut out squares of coloured paper using a guillotine or paper cutter. These shapes can then be pasted into cards that already have a design cut out of them, such as a Christmas tree or plain rectangle. Remember, it is the process of being involved in an activity that is important, not just the end product.

Providing an opportunity to practise skills, make choices and have fun

People with physical and multiple disabilities require lots of practice in order to learn new skills. They also require a structured, consistent way of learning skills and for this reason it is important that sensory-focused activities are set up in a consistent manner with plenty of opportunity for repetition. Within these activities, provide opportunities to make choices, so that people can learn that they can have an effect on their physical and social environment.

Although such activities are structured, they are still set up in a way that allows people to have fun and enjoy the sessions. They are more likely to participate and learn if they are having fun.

Community inclusion

People with profound and multiple disabilities often spend their day in segregated settings such as day centres. However, there is no reason why they should not be accessing facilities in their local community. So, if a person is interested in coffee, for instance, provide opportunities for them to have coffee at their local cafe.

4

Assessment and Evaluation

This section gives a brief overview of assessments and the importance of evaluation. Examples of the sorts of assessment tools used can be found in Appendix 1 (engagement background questionnaire) and Appendix 2 (sensory assessment). For a more in-depth assessment, the Triple C checklists should also be used (see Chapter 2).

Assessment

The first stage when assessing a sensory-focused activity is to consider people in terms of their current sensory and cognitive status and their sensory thresholds.

Reasons to assess

Reasons to assess include the following:

- to provide a baseline (to enable support people to see whether or not the people they are working with have changed)
- to give support people ideas on what types of activity to try
- to let support people know whether to provide more or less sensory input in activities to help the person with whom they are working participate more fully
- to discover what people like and dislike
- to discover what skills people have, or do not have and need to learn
- to discover whether or not a person has a specific sensory deficit
- to discover a person's level of understanding.

We will now look at each of these in turn.

BASELINE ASSESSMENT

The baseline assessment looks at what people are doing now. It is a period of time during which a behaviour is observed and measured without any intervention or training.

Often people exhibit self-engagement behaviours, which need to be replaced with person and object engagement behaviours. During the baseline assessments, support people can note what self-engagement behaviours people are exhibiting and whether or not they engage with people and objects. If the sensory-focused activities are successful, support people will be able to see, when evaluation is carried out, that the people with whom they are working have changed in positive ways: self-engagement behaviours will have reduced, and person and object engagement behaviours will have increased.

PROVIDING IDEAS ON WHAT TYPES OF ACTIVITY PEOPLE MAY ENJOY

By noting the type of self-engagement behaviours people exhibit, support people may be able to get some idea of the type of stimulation people are seeking. (Use the self-engagement section of the engagement background questionnaire in Appendix 1 to help gather this information.) Once information on self-engagement behaviours has been collected, write in the 'sensory system' column of the questionnaire which sensory systems these self-engagement behaviours stimulate. Through careful observation, appropriate activities can be provided that stimulate the same sensory systems people use to stimulate themselves. For example, if a person rocks they may be seeking vestibular (movement) stimulation, which could be provided in a more appropriate way by offering sessions on a trampoline.

Video-taping people is an ideal method for recording behaviours. The tape can be analysed at a later date when there is time to observe small changes in behaviour. The forms in Appendix 3 have headings to remind people of the types of question to ask when looking at video tapes. The first form in Appendix 3 gives guidance on what is a self-engagement behaviour and what the different senses are; the second part of the form provides only the headings. The self-engagement analysis form in Appendix 3 gives more detail about the self-engagement behaviours; for example, what are the self-engagement behaviours, what system is this stimulating, what causes the self-engagement behaviours to stop, what system does this stimulate? There is also a heading for activity ideas, which would be based on the sensory system in which people appear most interested. Assessment can thus be used to help plan subsequent activities that have meaning for people.

Another way to assess what a person may be interested in is to carry out a sensory assessment. The sensory assessment in Appendix 2 divides stimuli into the different senses so that it is possible to discern the sensory system in which a person is most interested. This again gives an idea of what types of activity and object to use with the individual clients. For instance, if they like bells and appear to be using their auditory system, build on this strength by providing other objects that also produce sound. A convenient way to store sensory objects to use with people is in the form of 'sensory banks' (p.50).

Although using people's interests is a good starting point for activities, it is also important to provide multisensory stimulation. This is because one sense can help in the development of another, and most everyday activities will be of a multisensory nature.

DISCOVERING WHETHER TO PROVIDE MORE OR LESS SENSORY INPUT IN ACTIVITIES TO HELP THE PERSON PARTICIPATE MORE FULLY

Every person has their own sensory profile (i.e. whether they are easily overstimulated or need a greater degree of stimulation to take notice of the things around them). By drawing up a sensory profile, it is possible to get an idea of the degree of stimulation people can tolerate (e.g. lots of noise). By observing people in different environments it is also possible to see which of these they prefer. For example, some people may find large, noisy groups (such as a music group) overstimulating, so they either withdraw or increase their self-engagement behaviours. With careful observation it is possible to learn which sensory activities are most appropriate for each individual.

DISCOVERING WHAT PEOPLE LIKE AND DISLIKE

People should be observed in a natural environment, where no direct stimuli are offered, as well as in group activities and the multisensory room. This sort of observation gives support people information on when self-engagement behaviours increase or decrease. By creating a likes and dislikes list and looking at the sensory systems stimulated by these, a pattern often emerges, showing which sensory system people prefer to use. For example, all their likes may have a touch component or they may be things that are visually stimulating. (An example of a likes/dislikes form can be found in Appendix 6.)

DISCOVERING WHAT SKILLS PEOPLE HAVE, OR DO NOT HAVE AND NEED TO LEARN

People are not only assessed on their self-engagement behaviours, but also on their person engagement (person interaction) and object engagement behaviours. This gives information on the areas in which people are interested, what they are skilled at and which areas need to be developed. For example, if a person is only interested in people, use this interest to help them become more interested in objects as well.

DISCOVERING WHETHER OR NOT A PERSON HAS A SPECIFIC SENSORY DEFICIT

A sensory assessment plays an important role in ascertaining whether or not people have any sensory deficits, such as visual impairments. Through observing a person, visual deficits may be noticed. For example, a person may not see small things or notice only big bright things. They may also have problems picking up objects – either feeling around for them, or reaching past or not far enough when trying to pick up an object. If there are any concerns about a person's vision or hearing, or if they have not had an assessment for some time, they should be referred to a specialist agency.

DISCOVERING A PERSON'S LEVEL OF UNDERSTANDING

Cognitive assessments need to be carried out so that everyone is aware of a person's level of understanding and thus can present activities that are appropriate and have meaning for people. For example, if a person is operating at the Explore stage of the learning continuum they will fail at activities that require an understanding of problem solving. Such activities would have no meaning for them so they are likely to become bored and their self-engagement behaviours could increase. (Refer to Chapter 2 for more information on cognitive frameworks.)

It is also important to assess a person's level of communication so that interactions can take place on a meaningful level. This means that information can be presented in a way that they can understand and that support people can recognise how they express their preferences. For example, if a person is operating at an unintentional level, they will not understand two-step instructions. They could become very frustrated if they are asked to do something and do not understand the instructions. They could also become frustrated if people do not understand their attempts at communication.

How to assess

One approach to assessment is for support people and therapists to gather information using a range of checklists and video-based information. The best way forward is a team approach, where information is gathered from significant people in the life of the person who is being assessed. This information is then analysed by the therapists to determine the types of activity best suited to that person's needs.

The sensory assessment summary form (Appendix 8) is divided into sections related to different sensory systems. Examples of types of objects to use under each system have been included. There is a degree of overlap here, as some objects stimulate more than one sense.

The sensory assessment form is basically a stimulus-response form, where support people note how others respond to different stimuli. Where possible, stimuli should be presented within an activity so that they have more meaning for people. For example, people's responses to tactile stimuli can be assessed during a craft activity and reactions to auditory stimuli can be assessed during a music group. The assessment will take place over a number of weeks as it is best to assess people in the course of their everyday activities.

An example of how such forms can be used is outlined in the following section, which describes the author's own work in a 'skills enhancement unit'.

This was developed in response to the needs expressed by people working at day centres for adults with disabilities. They were being asked to provide sensory activities but had little or no training in how to present activities for people with profound and multiple disabilities.

It offers an example of how to provide sensory-focused activities, which incorporates a training component for support people and demonstrates how people with physical and multiple disabilities were given the opportunity to develop specific skills through participation in an intensive group activity within a predetermined time frame. The training component for support people helped them learn how to provide the sort of activities that enable people with physical and multiple disabilities to further develop skills.

An example of assessment: the skills enhancement unit

Aims

The aims of the programme are twofold, as described below.

I. ASSESSMENT AND TRAINING FOR PEOPLE WITH PHYSICAL AND MULTIPLE DISABILITIES

This includes:

- recording self-engagement behaviours, then trying to reduce them

- assessing a person's cognitive level of functioning and which sensory system(s) they prefer to use

- finding an activity or piece of equipment that people are motivated enough to want to use

- promoting communication

- once people are interested in an activity/object, working on promoting choice-making and 'more' responses

- teaching people the concept of cause and effect with objects and teaching them to use switches to turn on pieces of equipment

- increasing person and object engagement.

2. SUPPORT PERSON TRAINING

This includes:

- the theory behind sensory-focused activities and maximising participation

- practical work in providing sensory activities, based on the structure set out in Chapter 5

- teaching people to use their observational skills, writing down observable responses to the different stimuli presented during the sensory activity; these are then given a probable meaning such as like/dislike

- teaching people to write up their own activity plans to ensure that they provide an activity with sensory components and also maximise participation from group members.

Format of the sensory activity programme

The programme comprises sensory activity group work and individual sessions based in a multisensory room. A speech pathologist and an occupational therapist co-run the sensory activity groups at the skills enhancement unit. Each group is time limited: one day a week over 12 weeks. The programme is primarily open to anyone who is functioning at an unintentional level of communication. However, those operating at an early intentional (informal intentional) level are also considered. Support people accompany participants from a day service placement.

During the first two weeks people are assessed on an individual basis in the multisensory room. During the remainder of the programme they are assessed in a group situation.

It is a full-day programme, making everyday activities such as morning drinks and lunchtime a sensory experience as well as offering people the opportunity to make choices. For example, people are offered the experience and choice of different types of herbal tea as well as coffee and juices.

Each day also includes a structured sensory activity, which may be making a dip, different drinks, face masks or soap (see the activity ideas in Chapter 8). After lunch, people are offered, on the basis of need, an aromatherapy/massage session, footspa or some time in the multisensory room, which is set up for relaxation or activity. At the beginning and end of the day, people sit in a circle and are given the opportunity to say hello and goodbye to both support people and their peers in the group. This marks a clear beginning and end to the group as well as giving people the opportunity to practise their social interaction behaviours.

At the end of the programme, the team completes a sensory assessment summary form (see Appendix 8) for each individual. This form provides the basis for an individual profile, looking at likes and dislikes and how these are expressed. As people are introduced to new experiences, their responses to these should be added to their profiles. Copies of the summary forms are then sent to the day services and to people's homes, along with ideas on how to make the home environment and everyday activities sensorily focused.

The assessment procedure

The assessment procedure used at the skills enhancement unit was as follows.

1. Engagement background questionnaires (Appendix 1) and interest charts (Appendix 4) are filled in by support people at day and home environments. These are completed before the 12-week sensory programme.

2. An occupational therapist carries out a sensory profile assessment at home and day settings.

3. Therapists carry out individual assessments in the multisensory room at the beginning of the 12-week sensory programme.

4. Sensory activities are carried out for ten weeks and people's responses to stimuli recorded.

5. During the last two weeks of the programme, support people plan a sensory activity and have the opportunity to lead it under the supervision of the therapists. They are then given feedback on how appropriate the activity was and whether or not it was conducted in a way that enhanced participation for participants.

6. At the beginning of the programme, video-tapes are taken of people at rest (in their natural environment), during a greeting, during a sensory activity and at meal times. Videos are also taken of people during the final sensory activity group.

7. The videos and recording forms from the sensory activity groups are then analysed in relation to the following questions:

   ○ What sensory system does the self-engagement behaviour stimulate?

   ○ What sensory system does the person prefer to use?

   ○ When does the self-engagement behaviour cease/diminish?

   ○ What are people's sensory thresholds?

   ○ What types of person and object engagement behaviour are people exhibiting?

   ○ At what level of cognition and communication does the person function?

   ○ What are the person's likes and dislikes?

   ○ How does the person communicate their likes and dislikes?

The forms found in Appendices 5, 6 and 7 may be used to assist in video and sensory group analysis.

At the end of the assessment the sensory assessment summary form (Appendix 8) is filled in. This summary sheet is used to identify the person's level of cognition and whether or not they primarily engage with self or with people and objects. It can therefore be used to set objectives and later to evaluate whether or not people have changed. For example, self-engagement behaviours may have stopped and they may now be interacting with people, whereas before they ignored others.

In addition, the form summarises information on the skills the person has and which skills need to be developed; it also gives recommendations for activity ideas and the types of sensory group people enjoy. Copies of the summary forms are then sent out to day placement services and homes, along with the list of likes and dislikes (see Appendix 6) and the personal communication dictionary form (see Appendix 7).

Outcomes of the skills enhancement unit

Many of the support people who have attended the skills enhancement unit have subsequently established sensory-focused activities at their day services. They have an interest in carrying out structured, quality activities that result in improved outcomes for the people they support. By attending the unit, support people have also improved their observational and recording skills and gained a greater understanding of the aims of sensory-focused activities. They realise that they are facilitators not 'doers' during the programme and that it is important to allow people to explore, rather than rushing to finish a product. As a result of participation in sensory-focused activities support people have drawn up a list of the skills required to run these activities (Appendix 13).

The outcomes for people with physical and multiple disabilities have included increased vocalisation, a greater interest in objects and people, more frequent interactions and learning new skills. A comprehensive list of benefits arising from involvement in the programme can also be found in Appendix 13.

5

How to Structure Sensory-Focused Activities

One of the most important factors when working with people with physical and multiple disabilities is the attitude and approach of support people. A positive attitude is essential. It is also important to proceed slowly and allow people time to respond. However, support people must themselves respond immediately to any attempts to communicate or the communication behaviour will extinguish (Barber 1994).

When interacting with people it is important to watch for behaviours that could indicate that they want more of something they like and to respond to this. Instead of automatically assisting a person to have another sip of their drink, ask them if they want 'more'. Initially, people may not realise that when they do something (e.g. lift their head) it means 'more', but if carried out and responded to consistently they may learn this routine and its meaning. It is important to give people time to respond. It is all to easy to jump in too early and pre-empt what they were going to do; if this is done too often people will give up trying to communicate because they know that if they wait long enough their needs will be met.

It is important to get to know a person well so that their behaviours can be understood and responded to. However, support people should be careful to ensure that a person's body language is not misinterpreted. A frown may not necessarily mean that a person does not like something. For this reason, it is important to gather information from a variety of people so that there is a consensus as to what a body movement or facial expression means.

Also be aware that people's movements may be dictated by their physical disability. For example, if a person has severe scoliosis (curvature of the spine), it may mean that when they try to look at an object, they actually look away from it. Others may interpret this as a dislike, but this is the only movement the person has. It is therefore important to consult with therapy team members (occupational therapist, speech pathologist, physiotherapist) with regard to positioning, people's movements, visual status, hearing, positioning of objects and types of object to use. In this way, a fuller understanding of people can be gained and everyone can work with them in a consistent manner.

Support people must also have realistic expectations for those with whom they work, not expecting too much but, at the same time, not limiting their potential. Many people might not progress beyond the Explore or Organise stages of the learning continuum. However, it is important to ensure that, through attitudes and careful observation, they are given the opportunity to develop to their full potential. It is important to be patient and not expect great changes straight away. Even if people appear not to be responding it is still worth providing sensory experiences: people cannot make choices or form concepts about their world if they are not exposed to different stimuli.

The way a sensory-focused activity is structured is very important. People need to learn what is going to happen, so should be given as many cues as possible. It should also be ensured that a *consistent approach* is adopted by all support people involved in the activity.

General principles for structuring sensory-focused activities

1. If running the activity with a group, do not have more than five or six people, with two support people.

2. Select a theme/activity before the activity begins and ensure that everything required for the activity has been collected before starting.

3. Remember to keep the activity simple. If it is too complicated, the focus will shift away from people participating to getting the task finished.

4. Select a piece of music that is always on when people enter the room for the activity. This may help them to anticipate what is going to happen as they will learn to associate the music with the sensory activity. Remember to turn the music off once the activity has started.

5. Use a tangible symbol, such as an object symbol, rather than telling people they are going to do a sensory activity. This will have more meaning for people with unintentional communication as words may mean very little to them. Use these symbols to cue people into the fact that they are about to do a particular activity. Use a particular object to represent the activity, such as a wooden spoon attached to a board. People may learn to recognise this and associate it with the activity.

6. For an extra cue, wear the same perfume/aftershave, as smells are often associated with people or events.

7. Try to wear clothing that is not highly patterned. It is important that clothing provides a plain background to the objects being presented.

8. Check that people are comfortable. It is difficult to concentrate when in pain, too hot, too cold, etc.

9. Always start the activity by greeting everyone who will be participating in the activity and encourage them to acknowledge others in the group. This will assist them to increase social interaction with their peers.

10. Use the individual's name to gain his or her attention and get them to look at another person or to alert them to the activity.

11. Always talk to a person and let them know what is going to happen before doing anything.

12. For individuals who have difficulty concentrating on tasks, present very short sequences of activity. Follow each with a short rest period and then refocus their attention to the task. This will usually happen in groups: a person has a turn then waits until it is their turn again.

13. Respond to any behaviours initiated by the activity and record observations of people's responses to different stimuli. Make up a stimulus/response checklist of the different materials used in the activity and try to give meaning to the different responses (e.g. turning away, moving arms and/or vocalising may mean dislike). Examples of recording sheets are supplied in the appendices.

14. For support people to understand how those with whom they are working indicate likes and dislikes, the behaviours of the latter have to be consistent in many different situations and observed by different people, so that it is not just one person assuming that they know how a person indicates their preferences.

15. Repetition and consistency are vital to assist learning. People will begin to anticipate what is expected of them in a given situation. This leads to learning and, eventually, the ability to apply new skills to different situations. Repeating the way a person is involved in an activity needs to occur on a routine basis.

16. Carry out the activity, remembering that the process is just as important as the end product. Give people time to explore and experience the individual aspects of the overall activity. Offer a particular stimulus again if a person has not had enough time to experience it.

17. All activities should be carried out interactively. Assist a person to make the most of sensory experiences (e.g. co-actively feel the shape and texture of an orange if the person is unable to pick it up themselves). Do this by moving the object around in their hand, helping them to explore the different textures and feel the edges. Also, gently squeeze

their hand around the object. Draw people's attention to the different objects/ingredients used in the activity and let them know when you have finished with a particular object, and that the interaction has ceased.

18. End the activity by saying goodbye to the individuals in a group and assist them to say goodbye to their peers. This helps people to know that the activity has finished.

19. The following list offers some ideas about the types of thing to observe during sensory activities.

    (a) What causes self-engagement behaviours to stop?

    (b) Do people look at you, other people or objects?

    (c) Do people track moving objects (including people) with their eyes (e.g. follow left, right, up, down)?

    (d) Do people reach for objects?

    (e) What do people do with objects (e.g. throw them to the floor, explore them by licking, manipulating)?

    (f) Do they use objects purposefully and functionally?

    (g) What are the properties of the objects people like?

    (h) Do people vocalise when given an object or when interacting with people?

    (i) When do people's facial expressions/body movements change? What do you think this means?

    (j) How long do objects/people hold a person's attention?

20. To assist with organising sensory-focused activities, collect together resources in sensory banks (see below). Figures 5.1 and 5.2 illustrate examples of sensory banks.

Sensory banks

Sensory banks are a concept described by Flo Longhorn (1988). They are collections of different types of materials and equipment, categorised according to the different senses. For example, an auditory bank (like that in Figure 5.2) would contain objects that make sounds (e.g. wind chimes, musical instruments, paper that rustles when scrunched); a visual bank (like that in Figure 5.1) might include torches, tinsel and silver paper that glitters; a tactile bank could include a collection of tactile materials with different properties (e.g. hard, soft, furry, rough, crinkly, sticky).

Collect together objects that stimulate vision. These sensory banks can be subdivided into fluorescent, black and white, and shiny objects. Keep a list of objects taped to the inside of the lid.

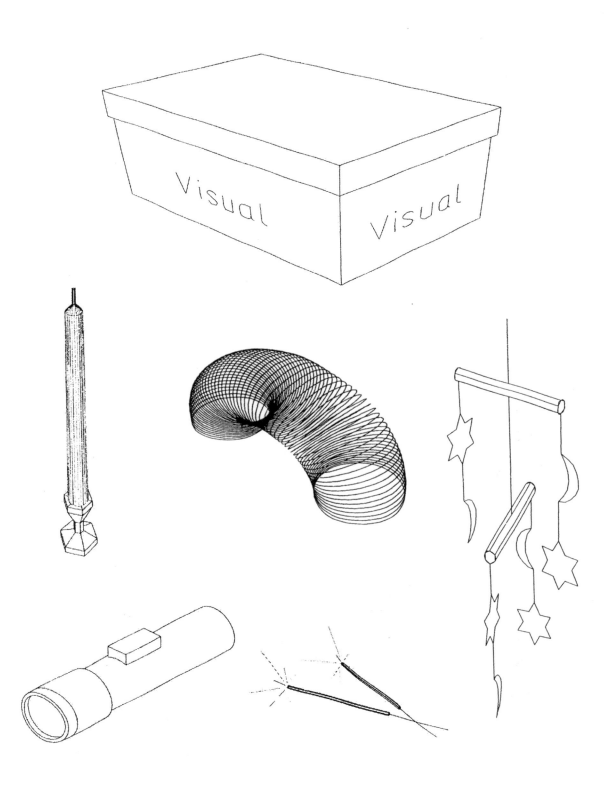

Figure 5.1 Visual sensory bank

Collect together objects that make different sounds. Keep a list of objects taped to the inside of the lid.

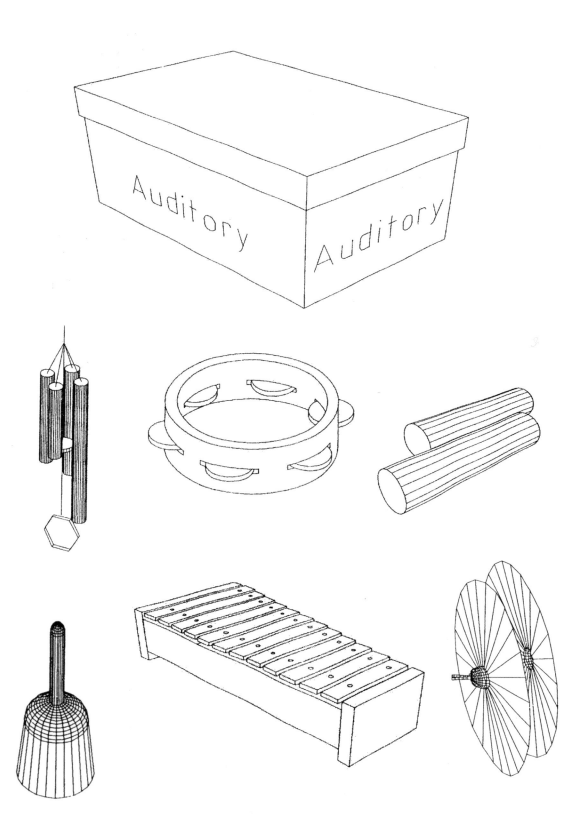

Figure 5.2 Auditory sensory bank

Sensory banks offer a useful way to store materials and are helpful when planning an individual activity. If a person is very motivated by visual objects, for example, you can explore the visual bank to find objects that will interest that person. Activity tables (like that in Figure 5.3) can be set up where visual objects are attached to a table or wheelchair (as in Figure 5.4) and the person can explore them at their leisure. An alternative to an activity table is an activity arch, which is a horizontal bar on two upright struts that can be positioned over someone's wheelchair or over a mat on the floor (as in Figure 5.5). Items can be attached to the arch and people then have the opportunity to explore the different objects in their own time.

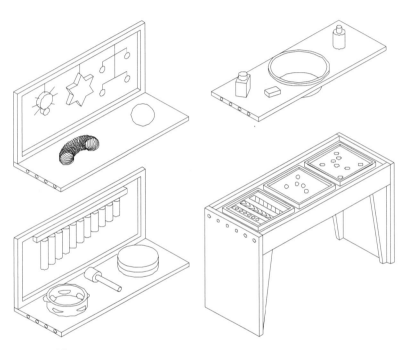

Figure 5.3 Activity tables

Activity tables have a variety of table-top activity insert panels. These panels are held securely in place with locking pins. Assist a person to co-actively explore objects on the activity table or set it up so that people can explore objects independently. Activity options are limitless. Examples include:

- mobiles and bright objects
- a musical instrument set up and ready for use
- a large basin for personal care objects (e.g. talc, soap, perfume)
- a large basin for objects to explore (e.g. shells, scarves)
- collage boards (e.g. braids, ribbons, buttons, marbles) with small objects sealed in netting so that people are unable to but them in their mouths
- large collages incorporating a variety of textures (e.g. textured fish; not shown).

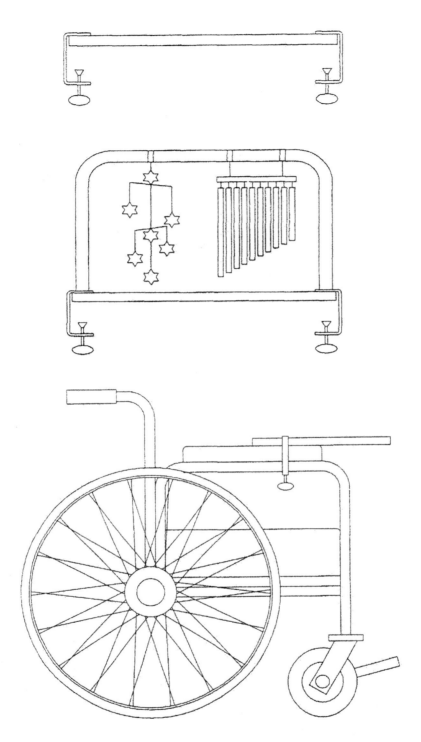

Figure 5.4 Clip-on activity tables

Clip-on activity tables can be made to attach to the arms of a person's wheelchair or their wheelchair tray. Objects are placed on the tray for people to explore (e.g. looking, listening, feeling, smelling, moving). A series of holes can be drilled in the table surface, enabling objects to be secured so that they will not fall out of reach if cast away. An overframe can be added to the table, enabling objects to be suspended.

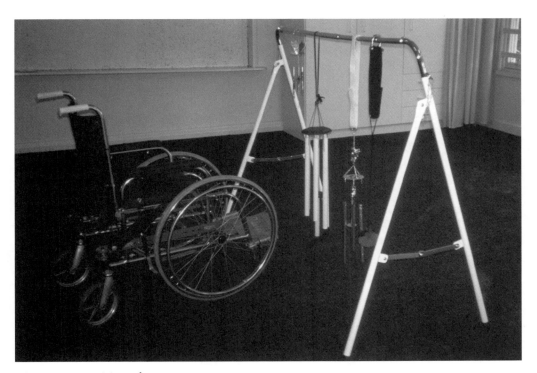

Figure 5.5 An activity arch

The materials in sensory banks can also be used for sensory activities. Thus a tactile collage could be made from the materials in the tactile bank, which may include different types of pasta, beans and rice. Obviously some of the categories overlap so that the pasta, beans and rice could also be used for an auditory activity if they were placed inside sealed tubes and tipped from one end to the other.

Sensory banks are also useful resources when planning sensory theme rooms or corners. People can be involved in creating their own sensory environments, such as an underwater corner or deep space room. Figure 5.6 shows some fish kites used in an underwater environment. These sensory environments can be planned as a long-term project. For example, one week people could explore the properties of the different types of paper used for the weeds, water, and so on; the next week they could explore the properties of different textures used to make sea creatures such as a fish, octopus or seahorse. You could also go to the beach and collect sand and shells for the room. Once the room is ready, set up a fan with a power box and switch, so that people can set the 'seaweed' moving themselves by operating the switch.

Large sensory environments often prove to be more stimulating than a maze of pin boards, small photographs and paintings, which are often visually very confusing. Figure 5.6 shows a sensory corner with an underwater theme. Large fish kites have been suspended in front of a curtain of silver streamers. A fan has been placed on a table behind the streamers. The fan can be attached to a power box and switch so that people can activate it. The wind from the fan causes the silver streamers to ripple gently and the fish to move.

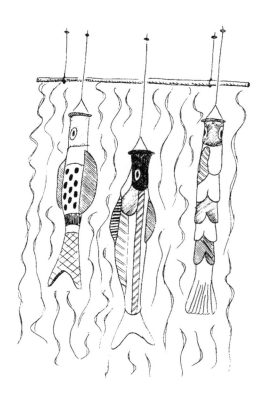

Figure 5.6 Sensory corner/sensory themes

Another example of a theme room is deep space. Different-textured mobiles could be made, as well as glittery and fluorescent mobiles of stars, planets and spaceships. Use a papier mâché activity to make rockets or planets. Moon craters can be made by mixing cornflour and water, or make coloured dough and use this to model objects for the deep space theme. Make a collage from rubbish, exploring the properties of the different cartons, plastic, cardboard tubes, and so on, and spray with gold or silver paint.

The following list gives some ideas for categories of sensory banks and the types of objects and materials that can be collected for them.

- **Auditory objects:** bells, whistles, hooters, shakers, musical instruments, cassette tapes (different types of music), pieces of paper that can be scrunched to make a noise (i.e. paper bags, hard paper, cellophane).

- **Olfactory objects:** peppermint foot lotion, strawberry lotions/bubble bath, perfumes, potpourri, apricot soap, incense, anything with a strong smell.

- **Gustatory objects:** make a list of the items you would like to use and include them in cooking activities. Include strong-tasting items and novel tastes such as yeast extract, avocado, garlic, lemon, Indian spices.

- **Indirect non-touch objects (air/water):** paper fan, hand-held fan, table fan, bicycle pump, squeezy bottle, plant spray, bubbles.

- **Soft tactile objects:** fur, feathers, silk, suede, mops, netting, lace, chiffon scarves, ribbons, polystyrene beads, soft brushes (shaving brush, blusher brush), carpet samples, bubble-wrap packing material, wool pompoms, different types of material.

- **Hard tactile objects:** fir cones, pieces of wood/bark, tins, beads, shells, broom heads, kitchen scourers, ridged wallpaper, corrugated cardboard, wooden foot massager, wooden egg, loofah.

- **Glittery, shiny objects:** glitter, silver objects, mirrors, diffraction paper, bike reflectors, holograms, torches, tinsel, silver foil.

- **Fluorescent objects:** glow-in-the-dark stars, fluorescent paint, fluorescent objects, ultraviolet (UV) lamp.

- **Moving objects:** mobiles, balls, bubbles, spinning objects, kites, remote-controlled cars.

- **Sensory boxes:** collect large containers (e.g. ice cream tubs) and fill them with different tactile materials, such as lentils, rice, shells, pasta, polystyrene balls, packing material, flour, strawberry blancmange mix.

To summarise, structured sensory activities provide the opportunity for people to make the most of the skills they have while also providing a learning environment. The aim is not necessarily to teach independence, but for people to be as independent as possible. This means that it is just as valid for people to participate partially in an activity where they need some help, such as co-active assistance to press a switch, as to carry out the task independently.

It is also important to maximise people's participation within their daily lives and local communities. Remember to include activities that occur within a person's daily life and give these a sensory focus. For example, if someone is motivated by olfactory objects, assist them to help in the garden or, if they are unable to do this independently, ensure that they are present when this activity is carried out. Also, instead of just offering plain tea or coffee, heighten the sensory components of this activity by offering different types of herbal tea or freshly ground coffee. As well as offering these activities at home or at a day centre/school, look for opportunities for people to take part in activities they enjoy within their local community.

Some people may appear to have reached a plateau in their development, but it is important to maintain their skills and to provide the opportunity for further experiences. Even if people do not appear to respond to different stimuli, they should still be given the opportunity to experience an enriched environment: they will have no opportunity to learn if we do not provide things of interest that may capture their attention. Appendix 10 is a list of equipment that people may find useful to have when conducting sensory activities.

PART TWO

ACTIVITY IDEAS

6

Introduction to Part Two

Part Two of this resource sets out a range of ideas for sensory-focused activities. It takes everyday activities and recipes and shows how they can be presented in a sensorily stimulating way, by emphasising the process and not just the end product.

Remember to take account of a person's sensory threshold when choosing activities; some people with low sensory thresholds, who become overstimulated easily, may be able to cope with the activities as they are presented in a structured way. The activities should also be repeated, perhaps changing some of the sensory properties but keeping the same process. This means that those taking part in the activities will be able to anticipate what will happen, which can reduce their anxiety. Other people may become so overstimulated that they will need to be involved in sensory activities on an individual basis.

In Chapter 7 there are some guidelines on how to make everyday activities sensorily stimulating so that sensory activities can be planned with this in mind. There are also useful templates with headings under which you can write up your own session plans, as well as examples of recording forms.

In Chapter 8, the activities themselves have been divided into the following sections:

- Drinks

- Food

- Personal and household care

- Art and craft.

When providing sensory-focused activities, make sure they are functional and meaningful to people. Think about ways to incorporate the activities and any skills learnt into everyday life. If teaching a person to turn on a light or food processor during a sensory-focused activity at a day setting, liaise with the home support people/family so that the person with a disability can also practise these skills at home. People are more likely to learn skills if they have meaning to them and they have the opportunity to practise.

To enable people with limited movement to participate in an active way, a power box and switch have been included in the activities. A power box is a remote-controlled power point with which special switches can be used to operate mains-powered appliances. This enables people to turn on a piece of electrical equipment (e.g. a food processor) even though they have limited hand use. If the individual has hand function, however, encourage them to use the switch/button on the electrical equipment itself rather than adding an external switch.

In preparation for the activities, it is recommended that two food processors be purchased. One can be used for drinks and food, and the other for personal and household care products, and art and craft activities.

If the person is unable to indicate their preferences, remember to note their behavioural responses to the different stimuli. This information can then be used to determine their likes and dislikes.

Before starting the activities, check that those with whom you will be working do not have allergies to certain foods, whether they are on particular diets or have specific medical conditions such as diabetes, and whether or not they are on medication. (Remember not to offer alcohol to people on medication.) Finally, check with a speech pathologist as to the types of food those doing the activities are able to eat (e.g. nuts and coconut are not suitable for people with swallowing difficulties).

Some of the activities use a UV lamp. Refer to Appendix 14 for precautions to consider when using such equipment. Appendix 10 lists equipment that it would be useful to purchase for use in sensory activities.

One last note of caution: if working with people who have a tendency to eat or drink *anything*, do not use those activities that involve poisonous substances (e.g. eucalyptus oil and aromatherapy oils). Also remember that supervision is required at all times, as some of the recipes involve sharp utensils or use small items, such as nuts, rice, lentils and sequins, which should not be swallowed.

7

Providing Sensory-Focused Activities and Maximising Participation

When planning sensory-focused activities, in order to maximise participation bear in mind the following guidelines.

1. Analyse the task/recipe and break it down into individual steps. Are there too many steps to the activity? If so, the focus will be on completing the end product not on the process of experiencing the sensory properties and maximising participation.

2. Look at each step and think about how it can be presented in a way that stimulates the senses. For example, is there anything to taste, smell, look at, listen to, feel?

3. Think how the individual steps can be presented to ensure that those doing the activity are given the opportunity to make choices. It may not be possible to offer choices at each step, but ensure that they are given the opportunity to make choices at various points throughout the activity.

4. Plan how the individual steps can be presented so that people can participate as much as possible in the task (e.g. by passing things to other people, putting rubbish in the bin, using a switch to operate a blender). Do not choose activities that require good hand skills, such as sticking sequins to a card, if those taking part in the activity are unable to do this.

When analysing a recipe or activity, look for as many opportunities as possible that will allow individuals to participate. For example, if a recipe includes grated cheese or ground almonds, don't buy grated cheese and ground almonds but help those taking part to grate and grind their own. When buying tins, don't buy ring-pull tins; buy tins that can be opened with an electric tin opener.

The following example – making a fruit smoothie – demonstrates how an activity can be presented in a sensorily stimulating way.

SENSORY STIMULATION

1. *Analyse the task: how to make a fruit smoothie*

   ○ Peel the fruit/open the packet (e.g. dried apricots).

   ○ Cut up the fruit.

   ○ Put the fruit in the blender.

   ○ Add milk or juice.

   ○ Blend the liquid and the fruit.

   ○ Drink the smoothie.

2. *How to make each step sensorily stimulating*

   ○ Peel the fruit/open the packet – before peeling the fruit, look at it, taste, smell, feel. Before opening the packet, pass it around to feel and listen to the sound it makes as it is crunched, then, once the packet is opened, smell, taste, feel the fruit.

   ○ Cut up the fruit – use an electric knife with a switch so that people can touch the switch to operate the knife. Encourage them to look at the fruit being cut up and listen to the noise of the knife.

   ○ Put the fruit in the blender – encourage the participants to watch as the fruit goes in.

   ○ Add milk or juice – before adding, touch the bottle/carton (if the juice/milk is kept in the fridge beforehand, individuals can feel how cold the container is). Look at, smell and taste the fruit and milk.

   ○ Blend the liquid and the fruit – put the blender in front of the participants so that they can see what is happening, hear the blender working, and reach out to touch the blender and feel the vibrations.

   ○ Drink the smoothie – encourage the individuals to look at, smell and taste the finished product.

3. *How to present the individual steps so that participants are given the opportunity to make choices*

   ○ Peel the fruit/open the packet – offer participants the opportunity to choose which fruit to peel or, if they are communicating unintentionally, offer different pieces of fruit to taste and observe their reactions to see which fruit they like and which they dislike.

   ○ Cut up the fruit – offer those taking part in the activity the choice of which fruit to cut, and whether or not they want to operate the knife.

   ○ Put the fruit in the blender – allow the participants to choose which fruit to put in.

   ○ Add milk or juice – offer individuals the choice of juice or milk for their smoothie. If anyone is communicating unintentionally observe their reactions when they taste the milk and juice to see which they prefer.

○ Blend the liquid and the fruit – offer people the choice of whether or not they want to operate the blender.

○ Drink the smoothie – offer participants the opportunity to taste the different smoothies (e.g. milk or juice) or, if anyone is communicating unintentionally, offer the different types of smoothies and observe which they appear to prefer.

4. *How to present the individual steps so that individuals can participate in the task*

○ Peel the fruit/open the packet (e.g. dried apricots) – co-actively assist people to pass the fruit/packet around the group and to put rubbish in the bin.

○ Cut up the fruit – if anyone is unable to hold the electric knife, use it with a power box and switch.

○ Put the fruit in the blender – co-actively assist participants to put the fruit in the blender.

○ Add milk or juice – co-actively assist those taking part to pass milk/juice containers around the group to explore; put the liquids in a small jug and co-actively assist them to pour milk/juice into the blender.

○ Blend the liquid and the fruit – if anyone is unable to use the switch on the blender, operate it with a power box and external switch.

○ Drink the smoothie – co-actively assist the participants to pour the drink into their cups, using a small, lightweight jug.

This approach to planning activities to ensure a sensory focus and maximise participation is useful with a range of activities. To help you plan activities by breaking them down in a similar way, you might like to photocopy and use the template on the following page.

On the pages that follow it you will find other templates and examples of recording forms that you can photocopy and use in conjunction with the activities in Chapter 8 or those you have devised yourself.

✓

Providing Sensory-Focused Activities and Maximising Participation

1. Analyse the task and break it down into small steps.

2. Make each step sensorily stimulating (taste, feel, smell, etc.).

3. Offer participants the opportunity to make choices.

4. Encourage participation at each step – importance of co-active assistance and partial participation.

Activity Sheet 1

(Use to set out activity plan)

Name of activity

Aims

Ingredients and equipment

Method

✓

Activity Sheet 2

(Use to set out activity plan)

Name of activity

Aims

Ingredients and equipment

Method

Example of a Recording Form 1

Name: _____   **Date:** _____

Activity: _____

1. Greetings/person engagement

Stimulus	Response	What do you think it means?
Called name		
Offered hand		
Touched person in greeting		
Looked at person – gave eye contact?		
Changes in vocalisations		
Watches/tracks people		
Person initiates contact		

✓

2. Note any self-engagement behaviours

_____

_____

_____

3. Reaction to ingredients and materials

Stimulus	Response	What do you think it means?

4. Reaction to electrical equipment
(e.g. food processor, electric knife – looked, listened?)

Stimulus	Response	What do you think it means?

5. Switch use

Used switch?	Yes	No
Which switch did the person use?		
Method of use?	Independent	Co-active
Wanted to use switch again?	Yes	No
Understood cause and effect?	Yes	No

✓

Which part of the body was used to activate the switch?	Right	Left
Hand		
Head		
Foot		
Other		

6. Comments

Example of a
Recording Form 2

Name: _____   **Date:** _____

Activity: Making hummus

1. Greetings/person engagement

Stimulus	Response	What do you think it means?
Called name		
Offered hand		
Touched person in greeting		
Looked at person – gave eye contact?		
Changes in vocalisations		
Watches/tracks people		
Person initiates contact		

✓

2. Note any self-engagement behaviours

_____

_____

_____

3. Reaction to ingredients and materials

Stimulus	Response	What do you think it means?
Chickpeas		
Garlic		
Tahini		
Lemon		
Paprika		
Hummus		

4. Reaction to electrical equipment
(e.g. food processor, electric knife – looked, listened?)

Stimulus	Response	What do you think it means?
Electric can opener		
Electric knife		
Electric juice extractor		
Electric food processor		

5. Switch use

Used switch?	Yes	No
Which switch did the person use?		
Method of use?	Independent	Co-active
Wanted to use switch again?	Yes	No
Understood cause and effect?	Yes	No

✓

Which part of the body was used to activate the switch?	Right	Left
Hand		
Head		
Foot		
Other		

6. Comments

8

The Activities

This chapter, which offers ideas for activities, is divided into four sections, as follows:

1.   Activities: drinks

2.   Activities: food

3.   Activities: personal and household care

4.   Activities: art and craft

Activities
DRINKS

APPLE AND CELERY JUICE

Aims

1. To provide a gustatory experience (variety of tastes).
2. To provide an olfactory experience (variety of smells).
3. To provide a tactile experience (variety of textures/vibrations).
4. To provide an auditory experience (sound of the electrical equipment).
5. To encourage an interactive environment.
6. To encourage participation in the activity.
7. To provide an opportunity to express likes and dislikes.
8. To provide an opportunity to make choices.
9. To encourage participants to use a switch and teach them the concept of cause and effect.
10. To have fun.

Ingredients and equipment

- 4 sticks of celery
- 8 apples
- Electric knife
- Electric juicer
- Power box

- Switches
- Chopping board
- Cups
- Spoons

Method

1. Position group members so that they have the opportunity to greet one another, either by looking at or reaching out to each other.
2. Pass around celery for them to smell and feel.
3. Pass around apple for them to smell and feel.
4. Place the celery and apple on the chopping board, then – using the electric knife with the power box and switch – cut them up. Pass around to taste, unless participants have eating difficulties.
5. Juice the celery in the electric juicer, placing participants' hands on the juicer or table to feel the vibrations. Be aware that some celery is very stringy and the juicer may have difficulty juicing it.
6. Pour the celery juice into cups and pass it around to taste.
7. Juice the apples in the electric juicer, placing participants' hands on the juicer or table to feel vibrations.
8. Pour the apple juice into cups and pass it around to taste.
9. Mix the apple and celery juice and pass it around in cups to taste.
10. Note whether individuals have a preference for the individual juices or the combination.
11. At the end of the activity, position group members so that they have the opportunity to say goodbye to one another, either by looking at or reaching out to each other.

APPLE, PEAR AND STRAWBERRY JUICE

Aims

1. To provide a gustatory experience (variety of tastes).
2. To provide an olfactory experience (variety of smells).
3. To provide a tactile experience (variety of textures/vibrations/temperatures).
4. To provide an auditory experience (sound of the electrical equipment).
5. To encourage an interactive environment.
6. To encourage participation in the activity.
7. To provide an opportunity to express likes and dislikes.
8. To provide an opportunity to make choices.
9. To encourage participants to use a switch and teach them the concept of cause and effect.
10. To have fun.

Ingredients and equipment

- Punnet of strawberries
- 3 pears
- 3 apples
- Yoghurt
- Ice cream
- Electric knife
- Electric juicer
- Electric food processor
- Power box
- Switches
- Chopping board
- Cups
- Spoons

Method

1. Position group members so that they have the opportunity to greet one another, either by looking at or reaching out to each other.
2. Pass around the fruit for them to feel and smell.
3. Place the various fruits on the chopping board, then – using the electric knife with the power box and switch – cut them up. Pass around to taste unless participants have eating difficulties or are allergic to strawberries.
4. Juice the pears in the electric juicer, placing participants' hands on the juicer or table to feel vibrations.
5. Pour the pear juice into cups and pass it around to taste.
6. Juice the apples in the electric juicer, placing participants' hands on the juicer or table to feel vibrations.
7. Pour the apple juice into cups and pass it around to taste.
8. Put the strawberries and any leftover pear and apple juice into the food processor.
9. Blend the fruit and juice, placing participants' hands on the electric food processor or the table to feel the vibrations.
10. Pour some of the juice into cups and pass around to taste.
11. Keep back some of the juice and experiment by adding yoghurt or ice cream to the mixture.
12. Put the yoghurt or ice cream mixture into cups and pass around to taste.
13. Note whether individuals have a preference for the individual juices, the combination or the yoghurt/ice cream mixture.
14. At the end of the activity, position group members so that they have the opportunity to say goodbye to one another, either by looking at or reaching out to each other.

CHILLED CHOCOLATE

Aims

1. To provide a gustatory experience (variety of tastes).
2. To provide an olfactory experience (variety of smells).
3. To provide a tactile experience (variety of textures/vibrations/temperatures).
4. To provide an auditory experience (sound of the electrical equipment).
5. To encourage an interactive environment.
6. To encourage participation in the activity.
7. To provide an opportunity to express likes and dislikes.
8. To provide an opportunity to make choices.
9. To encourage participants to use a switch and teach them the concept of cause and effect.
10. To have fun.

Ingredients and equipment

- 6 rounded tbsp caster sugar
- ¼ pint (125 ml) water
- 4 rounded tbsp cocoa powder
- 1 pint (½ litre) chilled milk
- 3 scoops vanilla or chocolate ice cream
- Power box
- Switches
- Electric frying pan
- Electric food processor
- Cups
- Bowls
- Spoons

Method

1. Position group members so that they have the opportunity to greet one another, either by looking at or reaching out to each other.
2. Place sugar in two bowls and pass around for participants to feel and taste.
3. Put sugar and water in the electric frying pan and use the power box and switch to turn it on. Place on low heat and stir until the sugar has dissolved.
4. Bring to the boil and simmer for 1 minute.
5. Pour cocoa powder into two bowls and pass around for participants to feel and taste. Note their reactions.
6. Pour the sugar and water syrup into the bowl of the electric food processor and add the cocoa powder. Use the electric food processor with power box and switch to mix in the cocoa powder.
7. Pass around some of the hot/warm chocolate sauce to taste.
8. Pass around some milk to taste.
9. Add the milk to the chocolate sauce in the food processor.
10. Use the power box and switch with the food processor to mix together the chocolate sauce and milk. Place participants' hands on the processor or table to feel the vibrations.
11. Pass ice cream around to taste.
12. Pour the mixture into cups and add ice cream. Offer to participants to taste.
13. At the end of the activity, position group members so that they have the opportunity to say goodbye to one another, either by looking at or reaching out to each other.

COCONUT BANANA DRINK

Aims

1. To provide a gustatory experience (variety of tastes).
2. To provide an olfactory experience (variety of smells).
3. To provide a tactile experience (variety of textures/temperatures).
4. To provide an auditory experience (sound of the electrical equipment).
5. To encourage an interactive environment.
6. To encourage participation in the activity.
7. To provide an opportunity to express likes and dislikes.
8. To provide an opportunity to make choices.
9. To encourage participants to use a switch and teach them the concept of cause and effect.
10. To have fun.

Ingredients and equipment

- 4 bananas
- Small tin of coconut milk
- Raw sugar (to taste) or honey
- Electric knife
- Electric tin opener
- Electric food processor
- Electric frying pan

- Power box
- Switches
- Chopping board
- Cups
- Bowls
- Spoons

Method

1. Position group members so that they have the opportunity to greet one another, either by looking at or reaching out to each other.
2. Pass around banana for them to feel and smell.
3. Place the banana on the chopping board and – using the electric knife with the power box and switch – cut it into pieces. Pass around to taste.
4. Open the tin of coconut milk using the electric tin opener.
5. Pour some coconut milk into cups and pass around to taste.
6. Put sugar into bowls and pass around to feel and taste, or pass honey around to taste.
7. Put all ingredients into the electric food processor and mix (using either honey or raw sugar). Place participants' hands on the appliance or table to feel the vibrations.
8. Divide in half and pass around some of the cold drink to smell and taste.
9. Heat the remainder of the mixture in the electric frying pan then pour into cups. Pass around for participants to taste the hot drink.
10. Note whether individuals have a preference for the hot or cold drink.
11. At the end of the activity, position group members so that they have the opportunity to say goodbye to one another, either by looking at or reaching out to each other.

COFFEE

(Ground coffee, cinnamon coffee, iced coffee, coffee and chocolate.)

Aims

1. To provide a gustatory experience (variety of tastes).
2. To provide an olfactory experience (variety of smells).
3. To provide a tactile experience (variety of textures/temperatures).
4. To provide an auditory experience.
5. To encourage an interactive environment.
6. To encourage participation in the activity.
7. To give participants the opportunity to make choices.
8. To provide an opportunity to express likes and dislikes.
9. To encourage participants to use a switch and teach them the concept of cause and effect.
10. To have fun.

Ingredients and equipment

- Coffee beans
- Brandy/rum essence
- Sugar
- Milk/cream
- 1 orange
- 1 lemon
- Cinnamon sticks/ground cinnamon
- Ice cream
- Chocolate powder
- Hot water/milk

- Electric coffee grinder
- Electric knife
- Electric frying pan
- Electric juicer
- Power box
- Switches
- Percolator/cafetière
- Bowl
- Chopping board
- Spoons

Method

1. Position group members so that they have the opportunity to greet one another, either by looking at or reaching out to each other.
2. Pour coffee beans into bowls and pass around to explore (smell, feel, listen).
3. If using an electric grinder, grind the beans using power box and switch. Place participants' hands on the appliance or table to feel the vibrations. Note participants' reactions to the sound of the beans being ground.
4. Put some ground beans in a bowl for them to feel and smell.
5. Make up coffee in the percolator/cafetière.
6. Offer the smell/taste of black coffee, coffee with milk/cream, sugar and no sugar.
7. Pass around orange and lemon for participants to feel and smell.
8. Using the electric juicer, squeeze the juice from the orange, then rinse out the juicer and squeeze the juice from the lemon, keeping the juices separate.
9. Pass juice around to smell and taste; note whether individuals indicate a preference.
10. Using the power box, switch and electric knife, place the orange and lemon on the chopping board and cut off the peel. Pass it around to feel and smell.
11. Pass around brandy/rum essence to smell and taste. Note participants' responses to see if they indicate a preference.

12. Place coffee in the electric frying pan and add brandy/rum essence, then the cinnamon, orange/lemon peel and sugar. Boil the mixture. Make up a selection of coffees according to participants' preferences for peel and essence.

13. Pass around ice cream to taste. Use it to make up iced coffees.

14. Mix up the chocolate powder with hot water and/or milk according to the instructions.

15. Blend this chocolate mix with coffee, water and milk or cream.

16. Compare participants' reactions to chocolate, coffee and the chocolate-coffee mix.

17. At the end of the activity, position group members so that they have the opportunity to say goodbye to one another, either by looking at or reaching out to each other.

This activity can be spread over different days as there is too much to get through in one session.

FRUITADE

Aims

1. To provide a gustatory experience (variety of tastes).
2. To provide an olfactory experience (variety of smells).
3. To provide a tactile experience (variety of textures/vibrations).
4. To provide an auditory experience (sound of the electrical equipment).
5. To encourage an interactive environment.
6. To encourage participation in the activity.
7. To provide an opportunity to express likes and dislikes.
8. To provide an opportunity to make choices.
9. To encourage participants to use a switch and teach them the concept of cause and effect.
10. To have fun.

Ingredients and equipment

- 1 orange
- 1 lemon
- 1 grapefruit
- ½ oz (15 g) citric acid
- 1 lb (500 g) sugar
- 1 pint water (boiling)
- Electric grater
- Electric juicer
- Electric food processor with blender
- Power box
- Switches
- Chopping board
- Sieve
- Cups
- Spoons
- Bottles
- Bowl
- Jug

Method

1. Position group members so that they have the opportunity to greet one another, either by looking at or reaching out to each other.
2. Score the lemon, orange and grapefruit and pass around to feel and smell.
3. On the chopping board, using the electric grater with power box and switch, grate the rind off the fruits.
4. Using the electric juicer with power box and switch, squeeze the juice out of the fruits, placing participants' hands on the juicer or table to feel the vibrations.
5. Pass the juices around to smell and taste. Note individuals' reactions.
6. Place the juices and rinds in the electric food processor. Add the citric acid and sugar to taste: to make the fruitade more tart, add less sugar.
7. Using the food processor with power box and switch, mix the ingredients together.
8. Place the mixture in a bowl, pour boiling water onto it and set aside to cool.
9. When the fruitade is cold, strain it through a sieve to remove the rind.
10. Pour into bottles, using a jug.
11. Pour the fruitade into cups and co-actively pour in cold water to dilute.
12. At the end of the activity, position group members so that they have the opportunity to say goodbye to one another, either by looking at or reaching out to each other.

FRUIT SMOOTHIE

Aims

1. To provide a gustatory experience (variety of tastes).
2. To provide an olfactory experience (variety of smells).
3. To provide a tactile experience (variety of textures/vibrations/temperatures).
4. To provide an auditory experience (sound of the electrical equipment).
5. To encourage an interactive environment.
6. To encourage participation in the activity.
7. To provide an opportunity to express likes and dislikes.
8. To provide an opportunity to make choices.
9. To encourage participants to use a switch and teach them the concept of cause and effect.
10. To have fun.

Ingredients and equipment

- 1 carton each of juice/milk (chilled)
- Different kinds of fruit (e.g. orange, banana, apple, watermelon)
- Electric food processor with blender
- Electric knife
- Power box

- Switches
- Chopping board
- Small jug
- Cups
- Spoons

Method

1. Position group members so that they have the opportunity to greet one another, either by looking at or reaching out to each other.
2. Encourage each participant to smell and feel each different type of fruit, one piece at a time, then pass it on to the next person.
3. Connect the electric knife to the power box and switch and, using the chopping board, chop the fruit into pieces.
4. Connect the electric food processor to the power box and switch and grate the apple. Place participants' hands on the food processor or table to feel the vibrations.
5. Co-actively pass around bowls of fruit to taste the different types of fruit – note individuals' reactions.
6. Pass the milk and fruit juice cartons around so that the group members can feel how cold they are.
7. Offer milk and fruit juice to taste. Note participants' reactions.
8. Connect the electric blender to the power box and use a switch to blend the fruit with the fruit juice or milk, according to group members' preferences.
9. Assist participants to pour the fruit smoothie mix into their cups, to smell and taste. Note their reactions.
10. At the end of the activity, position group members so that they have the opportunity to say goodbye to one another, either by looking at or reaching out to each other.

HOT CHOCOLATE MALT

Aims

1. To provide a gustatory experience (variety of tastes).
2. To provide an olfactory experience (variety of smells).
3. To provide a tactile experience (variety of textures).
4. To provide an auditory experience (sound of the electrical equipment).
5. To encourage an interactive environment.
6. To encourage participation in the activity.
7. To provide an opportunity to express likes and dislikes.
8. To provide an opportunity to make choices.
9. To encourage participants to use a switch and teach them the concept of cause and effect.
10. To have fun.

Ingredients and equipment

- 2 tbsp malted milk
- 1½ tbsp cocoa
- 2 cups milk
- 1½ tbsp honey
- Cream
- Power box
- Switches

- Electric whisk
- Electric frying pan
- Electric blender
- Bowls/small jugs
- Spoons
- Cups

Method

1. Position group members so that they have the opportunity to greet one another, either by looking at or reaching out to each other.
2. Assist participants to pour malted milk into 2 bowls. Pass one around to feel and the other to smell and taste.
3. Assist participants to pour cocoa into 2 bowls and pass around to feel, smell and taste.
4. Assist participants to pour milk into cups to taste.
5. Pass honey around to taste.
6. Pass cream around to taste.
7. Whip the cream with the electric whisk using the power box and switches.
8. Assist participants to pour milk into the electric frying pan. Turn on the frying pan using power box and switch. Bring to the boil and stir.
9. Put malted milk, cocoa, honey and hot milk into the electric blender. Mix using the power box and switch. Place participants' hands on the appliance or table to feel the vibrations.
10. Pour milk into cups; top with whipped cream and drink. Note participants' reactions.
11. At the end of the activity, position group members so that they have the opportunity to say goodbye to one another, either by looking at or reaching out to each other.

HOT GINGER

Aims

1. To provide a gustatory experience (variety of tastes).
2. To provide an olfactory experience (variety of smells).
3. To provide a tactile experience (variety of textures/vibrations/temperatures).
4. To provide an auditory experience (sound of the electrical equipment).
5. To encourage an interactive environment.
6. To encourage participation in the activity.
7. To provide an opportunity to express likes and dislikes.
8. To provide an opportunity to make choices.
9. To encourage participants to use a switch and teach them the concept of cause and effect.
10. To have fun.

Ingredients and equipment

- 1¾ oz (50 g) caster sugar
- 1 tsp ground ginger
- Bag of apples
- 6 oranges
- ½ pint (¼ litre) water
- Electric knife
- Electric juicer

- Electric food processor/blender
- Electric frying pan
- Power box
- Switches
- Chopping board
- Cups
- Spoons

Method

1. Position group members so that they have the opportunity to greet one another, either by looking at or reaching out to each other.
2. Pass sugar around for them to taste and feel.
3. Pass ginger around for them to smell and feel.
4. Put the sugar, ginger and water in the electric frying pan, operating it with the power box and switch, and heat slowly to dissolve the sugar. Bring to the boil, then simmer for 10 minutes.
5. Meanwhile, pass apple around to smell and feel.
6. Using the chopping board and electric knife, with the power box and switch, score the oranges to release the smell and pass around to smell and feel.
7. Again, using the chopping board, electric knife, power box and switch, cut the apples and juice them in the electric juicer. Place participants' hands on the juicer or table to feel the vibrations.
8. Pour the apple juice into cups and pass around to smell and taste.
9. Cut the oranges, using the electric knife, power box and switch, and juice in juicer. Place participants' hands on the juicer or table to feel the vibrations.
10. Pass orange juice around to taste.
11. Place all ingredients in the electric food processor/blender and mix.
12. Pour the finished drink into cups and pass around to taste and smell.
13. At the end of the activity, position group members so that they have the opportunity to say goodbye to one another, either by looking at or reaching out to each other.

HOT LEMON

Aims

1. To provide a gustatory experience (variety of tastes).
2. To provide an olfactory experience (variety of smells).
3. To provide a tactile experience (variety of textures).
4. To provide an auditory experience (sound of electrical equipment).
5. To encourage an interactive environment.
6. To encourage participation in the activity.
7. To provide an opportunity to express likes and dislikes.
8. To provide an opportunity to make choices.
9. To encourage participants to use a switch and teach them the concept of cause and effect.
10. To have fun.

Ingredients and equipment

- Oatmeal, medium (2 oz (57 g) for recipe)
- Raw brown sugar (1 tbsp (15 ml) for recipe)
- 1 lemon
- ½ pint (¼ litre) water
- 1 orange (optional)
- Electric juicer
- Electric knife
- Electric blender
- Power box
- Switches
- Jug
- Sieve
- Bowls
- Chopping board
- Spoons

Method

1. Position group members so that they have the opportunity to greet one another, either by looking at or reaching out to each other.
2. Score the lemon and pass around to feel and smell.
3. Using the electric juicer with power box and switch, squeeze the lemon.
4. Pass around some of the juice for participants to smell and taste.
5. Using the chopping board and electric knife with power box and switch, cut the lemon rind into pieces.
6. Put the oatmeal and sugar in bowls and pass around to feel.
7. Add the lemon juice and rind to the oatmeal and sugar.
8. Boil the water, add it to the ingredients and mix in the blender. Place participants' hands on the appliance or table to feel the vibrations.
9. Pour into a jug, cover and leave to cool.
10. When the drink has cooled, strain it through a sieve to remove the rind.
11. Pour the drink into cups and add water to dilute to taste.
12. At the end of the activity, position group members so that they have the opportunity to say goodbye to one another, either by looking at or reaching out to each other.

Orange juice can be added along with the lemon juice as a variation. Remember to pass the orange and its juice around to feel, smell and taste.

ICED MOCHA

Aims

1. To provide an olfactory experience (variety of smells).
2. To provide a gustatory experience (variety of tastes).
3. To provide a tactile experience (variety of textures/temperatures).
4. To provide an auditory experience (sound of the electrical equipment).
5. To encourage an interactive environment.
6. To encourage participation in the activity.
7. To provide an opportunity to express likes and dislikes.
8. To provide an opportunity to make choices.
9. To encourage participants to use a switch and teach them the concept of cause and effect.
10. To have fun.

Ingredients and equipment

- 1 tbsp cocoa
- 2 tbsp coffee
- 1½ tbsp sugar
- 2 tbsp hot water
- 2 cups milk
- 2 scoops ice cream
- Cream
- Chocolate
- Electric blender

- Electric beater
- Electric grater
- Power box
- Switches
- Bowls
- Spoons
- Small jugs
- Tablespoons

Method

1. Position group members so that they have the opportunity to greet one another, either by looking at or reaching out to each other.
2. Pass around the tin of cocoa powder to shake and feel.
3. Assist participants to pour cocoa into 2 bowls; pass 1 around to feel, the other to smell and taste.
4. Assist group members to pour coffee into 2 bowls and pass around to feel and smell. Add hot water to the coffee and pass around to taste.
5. Assist individuals to pour sugar into 2 bowls and pass around to feel, smell and taste.
6. Assist participants to pour milk into cups to taste.
7. Assist group members to pass around the ice cream container to feel the temperature and taste.
8. Assist participants to put the cocoa, coffee, sugar and water into the electric blender and, using power box and switch, mix the ingredients until sugar has dissolved. Place participants' hands on the appliance or table to feel the vibrations.
9. Add milk and ice cream, and blend until creamy.
10. Use the electric beater with power box and switch to whip the cream then pass around to taste.

11. Using the electric grater, grate the chocolate and pass around to taste.

12. Pour the drink into cups, top with the cream and grated chocolate – encourage participants to enjoy!

13. At the end of the activity, position group members so that they have the opportunity to say goodbye to one another, either by looking at or reaching out to each other.

KOSCIUSKO NIGHTCAP

Aims

1. To provide a gustatory experience (variety of tastes).
2. To provide an olfactory experience (variety of smells).
3. To provide a tactile experience (variety of textures/temperatures/vibration).
4. To provide an auditory experience (sound of the electrical equipment).
5. To encourage an interactive environment.
6. To encourage participation in the activity.
7. To provide an opportunity to express likes and dislikes.
8. To provide an opportunity to make choices.
9. To encourage participants to use a switch and teach them the concept of cause and effect.
10. To have fun.

Ingredients and equipment

- Chilled milk (1 cup milk for recipe)
- Orange rind
- 1 tbsp instant coffee
- 1 tbsp malted milk powder
- Electric blender
- Electric grater
- Electric frying pan
- Power box
- Switches
- Cups
- Spoons
- Small lightweight jug

Method

1. Position group members so that they have the opportunity to greet one another either by looking at or reaching out to each other.
2. Score the orange and pass it around for participants to smell and feel.
3. Using the electric grater with power box and switch, grate the rind of the orange. Pass the rest of the orange around to taste.
4. Pass the carton of milk around to feel.
5. Pour the milk into the jug, then co-actively assist someone to pour a cup of milk from the jug into the electric frying pan.
6. Add the orange rind and bring the milk to the boil.
7. Pour the milk into the electric blender and add the instant coffee and malted milk powder.
8. Using the power box and switch, blend until thoroughly mixed, placing participants' hands on the blender or table to feel the vibrations.
9. Co-actively pour the mixture into cups and pass around to taste. Note participants' reactions.
10. At the end of the activity, position group members so that they have the opportunity to say goodbye to one another, either by looking at or reaching out to each other.

LEMON NECTAR

Aims

1. To provide a gustatory experience (variety of tastes).
2. To provide an olfactory experience (variety of smells).
3. To provide a tactile experience (variety of textures/vibrations/temperatures).
4. To provide an auditory experience (sound of the electrical equipment).
5. To encourage an interactive environment.
6. To encourage participation in the activity.
7. To provide an opportunity to express likes and dislikes.
8. To provide an opportunity to make choices.
9. To encourage participants to use a switch and teach them the concept of cause and effect.
10. To have fun.

Ingredients and equipment

- 4 lemons
- 2 rounded tbsp caster sugar
- 2 rounded tbsp honey
- 1 pint (½ litre) boiling water
- Ice cubes
- Power box
- Switches
- Chopping board
- Electric knife

- Electric juice extractor
- Electric food mixer
- Mixing bowl
- Sieve
- Spoons
- Bowls
- Plastic bag
- Jug

Method

1. Position group members so that they have the opportunity to greet one another, either by looking at or reaching out to each other.
2. Using the chopping board and the electric knife with power box and switch, pare the rind off the lemons.
3. Pass some lemon rind around for participants to feel and smell. Place the rest in the mixing bowl.
4. Pour sugar into 2 bowls; pass 1 around for group members to feel the texture, and the other one to taste.
5. Pour honey into 2 bowls; pass 1 around for group members to feel the texture, and the other one to taste.
6. Place sugar and honey in the mixing bowl with the lemon rind.
7. Pour the boiling water into the mixing bowl and use the electric mixer with power box and switch to blend. Stir until the honey and sugar dissolve.
8. Strain the liquid through a sieve into a jug.
9. Use the electric juice extractor with power box and switch to squeeze the juice from the lemons, placing participants' hands on the juice extractor or table to feel the vibrations.
10. Pass juice around to smell and taste.
11. Add the juice to the jug.
12. Place the ice cubes in the plastic bag and pass around for participants to feel.
13. Divide the juice and add ice cubes to half. Offer hot/warm juice and ice-cold juice to taste. Note any individual preferences.
14. At the end of the activity, position group members so that they have the opportunity to say goodbye to one another, either by looking at or reaching out to each other.

ORANGE AND LEMON JUICE

Aims

1. To provide a gustatory experience (variety of tastes).
2. To provide an olfactory experience (variety of smells).
3. To provide a tactile experience (variety of textures/vibrations/temperatures).
4. To provide an auditory experience (sound of the electrical equipment).
5. To encourage an interactive environment.
6. To encourage participation in the activity.
7. To provide an opportunity to express likes and dislikes.
8. To provide an opportunity to make choices.
9. To encourage participants to use a switch and teach them the concept of cause and effect.
10. To have fun.

Ingredients and equipment

- 4 oranges
- 3 lemons
- Raw sugar
- Water
- Ice cubes
- Power box
- Switches
- Electric juicer

- Electric knife
- Chopping board
- Bowls
- Cups
- Spoons
- Plastic bag
- Small jug

Method

1. Position group members so that they have the opportunity to greet one another, either by looking at or reaching out to each other.
2. Pass oranges and lemons around to feel and smell (score the fruit first, to release the smell).
3. Using the chopping board and electric knife with power box and switch, cut the fruit in half or pieces, depending on the juicer used.
4. Juice the fruit using the electric juicer. Help participants to place their hands on the juicer or table to feel the vibrations.
5. Pass the different juices around to taste and note any preferences.
6. Put sugar in 2 bowls and pass around – one for tasting and the other for feeling.
7. Put the ice cubes in the plastic bag and pass around for group members to feel.
8. Add water and sugar to the juices, depending on taste. Experiment to see whether participants prefer more tart juice or sweeter juice.
9. Pour into cups and add ice cubes according to individual preferences.
10. At the end of the activity, position group members so that they have the opportunity to say goodbye to one another, either by looking at or reaching out to each other.

ORANGE TEA

Aims

1. To provide a gustatory experience (variety of tastes).
2. To provide an olfactory experience (variety of smells).
3. To provide a tactile experience (variety of textures/vibrations/temperatures).
4. To provide an auditory experience (sound of the electrical equipment).
5. To encourage an interactive environment.
6. To encourage participation in the activity.
7. To provide an opportunity to express likes and dislikes.
8. To provide an opportunity to make choices.
9. To encourage participants to use a switch and teach them the concept of cause and effect.
10. To have fun.

Ingredients and equipment

- 6 cloves for recipe, plus extra to feel
- Cinnamon sticks, 5 cm each, for recipe
- ½ oz (15 g) black tea, plus extra to feel
- 4 oz (113 g) sugar, plus extra to feel
- 5 oranges
- 1¾ pints (1 litre) cold water
- Ice cubes
- Plastic bag
- Electric knife
- Electric juicer

- Electric frying pan
- Power box
- Switches
- Chopping board
- Cups
- Spoons
- Bowls
- Jugs
- Tea strainer

Method

1. Position group members so that they have the opportunity to greet one another, either by looking at or reaching out to each other.
2. Put the cloves in the electric frying pan with the cold water. Bring to the boil and pour over the ½ oz (15 g) of tea.
3. Add sugar, stir and then strain into a jug, using the tea strainer.
4. Put the jug of tea into the fridge to chill.
5. Put the extra cloves, cinnamon sticks, extra black tea leaves and sugar into bowls and pass around for participants to feel and smell.
6. Score an orange and pass around for them to feel and smell.
7. Using the power box with switches, cut up the oranges on the chopping board with the electric knife, then put them in the electric juicer. Place participants' hands on the juicer or table to feel the vibrations.
8. Pass juice around to taste.
9. Put the ice cubes in the plastic bag and pass around for participants to feel.
10. Mix the spiced tea with the orange juice.
11. Add the ice cubes to make the drink colder.
12. Pour the finished drink into cups and pass around to taste.
13. At the end of the activity, position group members so that they have the opportunity to say goodbye to one another, either by looking at or reaching out to each other.

PASSIONFRUIT AND LEMON JUICE

Aims

1. To provide a gustatory experience (variety of tastes).
2. To provide an olfactory experience (variety of smells).
3. To provide a tactile experience (variety of textures/vibrations/temperatures).
4. To provide an auditory experience (sound of the electrical equipment).
5. To encourage an interactive environment.
6. To encourage participation in the activity.
7. To provide an opportunity to express likes and dislikes.
8. To provide an opportunity to make choices.
9. To encourage participants to use a switch and teach them the concept of cause and effect.
10. To have fun.

Ingredients and equipment

- 5 passionfruits
- 1 lemon
- 4 oranges
- Honey
- Electric knife
- Electric juicer
- Electric food processor
- Power box
- Switches
- Chopping board
- Cups
- Spoons

Method

1. Position group members so that they have the opportunity to greet one another, either by looking at or reaching out to each other.
2. Pass around the fruit for participants to feel and smell.
3. Using the chopping board and electric knife with power box and switch, cut the fruit into halves.
4. Juice the lemon in the electric juicer, placing participants' hands on the juicer or table to feel the vibrations.
5. Pass around some lemon juice to taste.
6. Juice the oranges in the electric juicer, placing participants' hands on the juicer or table to feel the vibrations.
7. Pass some orange juice around to taste.
8. Scoop the seeds out of the passionfruit and pass some of the fruit around to taste. Do not offer to participants who have eating difficulties.
9. Pass honey around to taste.
10. Put the passionfruit, lemon, oranges and honey, to taste, in the electric food processor and mix. Omit the passionfruit if participants have eating difficulties.
11. Pour the finished drink into cups and pass around to taste.
12. At the end of the activity, position group members so that they have the opportunity to say goodbye to one another, either by looking at or reaching out to each other.

PEANUT MILK

Aims

1. To provide a gustatory experience (variety of tastes).
2. To provide an olfactory experience (variety of smells).
3. To provide a tactile experience (variety of textures/vibrations/temperatures).
4. To provide an auditory experience (sound of the electrical equipment).
5. To encourage an interactive environment.
6. To encourage participation in the activity.
7. To provide an opportunity to express likes and dislikes.
8. To provide an opportunity to make choices.
9. To encourage participants to use a switch and teach them the concept of cause and effect.
10. To have fun.

Ingredients and equipment

- 1 cup cold milk
- 1 cup soy milk
- 1 tbsp smooth peanut butter
- 1 tsp honey
- Yoghurt or ice cream

- Electric food processor/blender
- Power box
- Switches
- Cups
- Spoons

Method

1. Position group members so that they have the opportunity to greet one another, either by looking at or reaching out to each other.
2. Pass the cold milk and soy milk around to feel and taste.
3. Pass peanut butter around to taste (do not use if any group member has a peanut allergy).
4. Pass honey around to taste and smell.
5. Place the cows' milk, peanut butter and honey in the electric food processor/blender and, using the power box and switch, mix. Place participants' hands on the equipment or table to feel the vibrations.
6. Pour the finished drink into cups and pass around to taste and smell.
7. Make variations by using soy milk instead and adding yoghurt or ice cream. Note which combination participants prefer.
8. At the end of the activity, position group members so that they have the opportunity to say goodbye to one another, either by looking at or reaching out to each other.

PINK GRAPEFRUIT JUICE

Aims

1. To provide a gustatory experience (variety of tastes).
2. To provide an olfactory experience (variety of smells).
3. To provide a tactile experience (variety of textures/vibrations).
4. To provide an auditory experience (sound of the electrical equipment).
5. To encourage an interactive environment.
6. To encourage participation in the activity.
7. To provide an opportunity to express likes and dislikes.
8. To provide an opportunity to make choices.
9. To encourage participants to use a switch and teach them the concept of cause and effect.
10. To have fun.

Ingredients and equipment

- 1 large pink grapefruit
- 1 lime
- Tonic water
- Mint leaves
- Honey
- Electric knife
- Electric juicer

- Electric food processor/blender
- Power box
- Switches
- Chopping board
- Cups
- Spoons

Method

1. Position group members so that they have the opportunity to greet one another, either by looking at or reaching out to each other.
2. Pass around fruit to smell and feel.
3. Pass around mint to smell and feel.
4. Using the chopping board and electric knife with power box and switch, cut the fruit into halves.
5. Juice the grapefruit in the electric juicer, placing participants' hands on the juicer or table to feel the vibrations.
6. Pass grapefruit juice around to taste.
7. Juice the lime in the electric juicer, placing participants' hands on the juicer or table to feel the vibrations.
8. Pass around lime juice to taste.
9. Put the mint leaves in the electric food processor/blender and chop. Pass around to smell.
10. Pass tonic water around to taste.
11. Put the juices, mint and tonic water in the food processor/blender and mix.
12. Put aside half of the mixture and pass the rest around to taste. It will have a very sharp taste.
13. Pass honey around to smell and taste.
14. Add honey to the other half of the finished drink to make it sweeter.
15. Pass this drink around to taste.
16. Note whether individuals have a preference for the sharper or sweeter drink.
17. At the end of the activity, position group members so that they have the opportunity to say goodbye to one another, either by looking at or reaching out to each other.

PUNCH

Aims

1. To provide a gustatory experience (variety of tastes).
2. To provide an olfactory experience (variety of smells).
3. To provide a tactile experience (variety of textures/vibrations/temperatures).
4. To provide an auditory experience (sound of the electrical equipment).
5. To encourage an interactive environment.
6. To encourage participation in the activity.
7. To provide an opportunity to express likes and dislikes.
8. To provide an opportunity to make choices.
9. To encourage participants to use a switch and teach them the concept of cause and effect.
10. To have fun.

Ingredients and equipment

- 4 grapefruits (as an alternative use pink grapefruits)
- Punnet of strawberries
- 2 oranges
- 1 small bottle of bitter lemon (cold)
- ¾ pint (½ litre) soda water (cold)
- Electric knife
- Electric juicer
- Electric food processor/blender
- Power box
- Switches
- Chopping board
- Cups
- Spoons

Method

1. Position group members so that they have the opportunity to greet one another, either by looking at or reaching out to each other.
2. Pass fruits around to feel and smell.
3. Put the strawberries in the electric food processor/blender and use with the power box and switch.
4. Pass crushed strawberries around to smell and taste.
5. Score the grapefruits and oranges to release the aroma, and pass around to feel and smell.
6. Using the chopping board and electric knife with power box and switch, cut the grapefruits and oranges into halves.
7. Juice the grapefruits in the electric juicer, placing participants' hands on the juicer or table to feel the vibrations.
8. Pass around some grapefruit juice to taste.
9. Juice the oranges in the electric juicer, placing participants' hands on the juicer or table to feel the vibrations.
10. Pass some orange juice around to taste.
11. Pass bitter lemon around to taste, smell and feel.
12. Pass soda water around to taste, smell and feel.
13. Place all ingredients in the food processor/blender and mix.
14. Pour the finished drink into cups and pass around to taste and smell.
15. At the end of the activity, position group members so that they have the opportunity to say goodbye to one another, either by looking at or reaching out to each other.

RASPBERRY FIZZ

Aims

1. To provide a gustatory experience (variety of tastes).
2. To provide an olfactory experience (variety of smells).
3. To provide a tactile experience (variety of textures/vibrations/temperatures).
4. To provide an auditory experience (sound of the electrical equipment).
5. To encourage an interactive environment.
6. To encourage participation in the activity.
7. To provide an opportunity to express likes and dislikes.
8. To provide an opportunity to make choices.
9. To encourage participants to use a switch and teach them the concept of cause and effect.
10. To have fun.

Ingredients and equipment

- Small punnet of frozen raspberries
- Fizzy mineral water
- 1 lemon
- 1 lime
- Honey
- Electric knife
- Electric juicer
- Electric food processor
- Power box
- Switches
- Chopping board
- Cups
- Spoons

Method

1. Position group members so that they have the opportunity to greet one another, either by looking at or reaching out to each other.
2. Pass the frozen raspberries around to feel the coldness.
3. Put the raspberries in the electric food processor and listen to the noise as they break up.
4. Pass crushed raspberries around to smell and taste.
5. Score the lemon and lime to release the aroma, and pass around to feel and smell.
6. Using the chopping board and electric knife with power box and switch, cut the lemon and lime into halves.
7. Juice the lemon in the electric juicer, placing participants' hands on the juicer or table to feel the vibrations.
8. Pass around some lemon juice to taste.
9. Juice the lime in the electric juicer, placing participants' hands on the juicer or table to feel the vibrations.
10. Pass some lime juice around to taste.
11. Pass fizzy mineral water around to taste.
12. Keep half the crushed raspberries aside and place the juices with the rest of the raspberries in the food processor, along with some mineral water.
13. Pour the drink into cups and pass around to taste. It will have a very tart taste.
14. Put the remaining raspberries in the food processor with the honey, to taste, and mineral water.
15. Pass around to taste.
16. Note whether individuals have a preference for the tart or sweet combination.
17. At the end of the activity, position group members so that they have the opportunity to say goodbye to one another, either by looking at or reaching out to each other.

SOY BANANA THICK MILKSHAKE

Aims

1. To provide a gustatory experience (variety of tastes).
2. To provide an olfactory experience (variety of smells).
3. To provide a tactile experience (variety of textures/vibrations/temperatures).
4. To provide an auditory experience (sounds of the electrical equipment).
5. To encourage an interactive environment.
6. To encourage participation in the activity.
7. To provide an opportunity to express likes and dislikes.
8. To provide an opportunity to make choices.
9. To encourage participants to use a switch and teach them the concept of cause and effect.
10. To have fun.

Ingredients and equipment

The following quantities make 1 blender of milkshake.

- 1 frozen banana (plus extra banana to feel)
- 1 cup soy milk
- 2 tbsp vanilla yoghurt
- 1 squeeze golden syrup
- A few cardamom pods
- 1 unseeded watermelon

- Electric blender
- Power box
- Switches
- Electric nut grinder or food processor
- Cups
- Spoons

Method

1. Position group members so that they have the opportunity to greet one another, either by looking at or reaching out to each other.
2. Pass the cold banana around to feel and taste.
3. Pass soy milk, vanilla yoghurt and golden syrup around to smell and taste.
4. Put the cardamom pods in the electric food processor/nut grinder and, using the power box and switch, grind to a powder.
5. Pass around to smell and taste.
6. Put all ingredients into the electric blender and mix well. Place participants' hands on the table or blender to feel the vibrations.
7. As a variation, add cubes of fresh watermelon to the mixture and blend well.
8. Pour the finished thick shake into cups and pass around to taste and smell.
9. At the end of the activity, position group members so that they have the opportunity to say goodbye to one another, either by looking at or reaching out to each other.

SPICY HOT CHOCOLATE

Aims

1.   To provide a gustatory experience (variety of tastes).
2.   To provide an olfactory experience (variety of smells).
3.   To provide a tactile experience (variety of textures/temperatures).
4.   To provide an auditory experience (sound of the electrical equipment).
5.   To encourage an interactive environment.
6.   To encourage participation in the activity.
7.   To provide an opportunity to express likes and dislikes.
8.   To provide an opportunity to make choices.
9.   To encourage participants to use a switch and teach them the concept of cause and effect.
10.   To have fun.

Ingredients and equipment

- Bar of plain cooking chocolate
- ¾ pint (½ litre) milk (or soy milk as an alternative)
- Nutmeg (1 tsp ground for recipe)
- Cinnamon (1 tsp ground for recipe)
- ¼ pint (125 ml) cream (cold)
- Electric knife
- Electric grinder

- Electric food processor/blender
- Electric whisk
- Electric frying pan
- Power box
- Switches
- Chopping board
- Cups
- Spoons

Method

1.   Position group members so that they have the opportunity to greet one another, either by looking at or reaching out to each other.
2.   Pass chocolate around in its packet to feel and listen to.
3.   Using the chopping board and electric knife with power box and switch, cut the chocolate into small blocks. Pass around to smell and taste, unless anyone has eating difficulties.
4.   Pass milk around to taste.
5.   Dissolve the chocolate in the milk over a low heat and simmer. When the mixture has cooled down pass it around to smell and taste.
6.   Meanwhile grind the nutmeg in the electric grinder, and pass around to smell.
7.   Grind the cinnamon in the electric grinder, and pass around to smell.
8.   Pass the cream pot around to feel and taste.
9.   Whip the cream with the electric whisk, and pass around to taste.
10.   Place the chocolate milk and spices in the electric food processor/blender and mix. Place participants' hands on the appliance or table to feel the vibrations.
11.   Using the electric frying pan, dissolve chocolate in milk over a low heat and simmer.
12.   Pour into cups and top with whipped cream. Pass around to smell and taste.
13.   At the end of the activity, position group members so that they have the opportunity to say goodbye to one another, either by looking at or reaching out to each other.

SPICY TOMATO

Aims

1. To provide a gustatory experience (variety of tastes).
2. To provide an olfactory experience (variety of smells).
3. To provide a tactile experience (variety of textures/vibrations).
4. To provide an auditory experience (sound of the electrical equipment).
5. To encourage an interactive environment.
6. To encourage participation in the activity.
7. To provide an opportunity to express likes and dislikes.
8. To provide an opportunity to make choices.
9. To encourage participants to use a switch and teach them the concept of cause and effect.
10. To have fun.

Ingredients and equipment

- 6–8 tomatoes
- 1 lemon
- Worcestershire sauce
- Tabasco sauce
- Electric knife
- Electric juicer
- Electric food processor/blender
- Power box
- Switches
- Chopping board
- Cups
- Spoons

Method

1. Position group members so that they have the opportunity to greet one another, either by looking at or reaching out to each other.
2. Pass a tomato around to smell and feel.
3. Using the chopping board and electric knife with power box and switch, cut the tomatoes into pieces.
4. Pass tomato around to taste – unless anyone has eating difficulties or is allergic to tomatoes.
5. Score the lemon to release the aroma, and pass around to feel and smell.
6. Juice the lemon in the electric juicer, placing participants' hands on the juicer or table to feel the vibrations.
7. Pass around some lemon juice to taste.
8. Pass around Worcestershire sauce and tabasco sauce to smell.
9. Put the tomatoes, a tablespoon of lemon juice, dash of Worcestershire sauce and dash of tabasco sauce into the electric food processor/blender and mix well.
10. Pour the finished drink into cups and pass around to smell and taste.
11. At the end of the activity, position group members so that they have the opportunity to say goodbye to one another, either by looking at or reaching out to each other.

Activities
FOOD

APRICOT AND ORANGE MOUSSE

Aims

1. To provide a gustatory experience (variety of tastes).
2. To provide an olfactory experience (variety of smells).
3. To provide a tactile experience (variety of textures/vibrations/temperatures).
4. To provide an auditory experience (sounds of the electrical equipment).
5. To encourage an interactive environment.
6. To encourage participation in the activity.
7. To provide an opportunity to express likes and dislikes.
8. To provide an opportunity to make choices.
9. To encourage participants to use a switch and teach them the concept of cause and effect.
10. To have fun.

Ingredients and equipment

- 1¼ cups (310 ml) apricot nectar
- 2 tsp caster sugar
- 1 tsp orange rind
- 3 tsp gelatine
- 4 tbsp orange juice
- 2 oranges
- ¾ cup (190 ml) evaporated skimmed milk, chilled
- Hot water
- Electric food processor/blender
- Electric grater
- Electric tin opener
- Electric juicer
- Electric knife
- Switches
- Power box
- Chopping board
- Bowls
- Spoons
- Dessert dishes/glasses

Method

1. Position group members so that they have the opportunity to greet one another, either by looking at or reaching out to one another.
2. Use the electric tin opener with power box and switch to open the tin of nectar.
3. Offer participants a taste of the nectar. Note their reactions.
4. Pour caster sugar into bowls for group members to feel and taste.
5. Pass the oranges around to feel and smell.
6. Using the chopping board and electric knife with power box and switch, cut the oranges into quarters and remove the rind.
7. Use the electric juicer to extract the orange juice. Place participants' hands on the juicer or table to feel the vibrations.
8. Fill a bowl with hot water.
9. Place the orange juice in another, smaller bowl and sprinkle the gelatine over it. Place this bowl in the hot water bowl until the gelatine dissolves.
10. Allow the gelatine mixture to cool for 5 minutes.
11. Using the electric grater with power box and switch, grate the orange rind.
12. Stir the apricot nectar, sugar and orange rind into the cooled gelatine mixture. Omit the rind if people have swallowing difficulties.
13. Use the electric tin opener with power box and switch to open the tin of skimmed milk.
14. Offer people a taste of the milk.

15. Use the electric food processor/blender to beat skimmed milk until it is thick.

16. Fold the milk into the apricot mixture, and offer participants a taste of the finished product.

17. Spoon into dessert dishes/glasses and refrigerate until set.

18. Offer group members the cold apricot and orange mousse.

19. At the end of the activity, position group members so that they have the opportunity to say goodbye to one another, either by looking at or reaching out to one another.

AVOCADO DIP

Aims

1. To provide a gustatory experience (variety of tastes).
2. To provide an olfactory experience (variety of smells).
3. To provide a tactile experience (variety of textures/vibrations).
4. To provide an auditory experience (sounds of the electrical equipment).
5. To provide an interactive environment.
6. To encourage participation in the activity.
7. To provide an opportunity to express likes and dislikes.
8. To provide an opportunity to make choices.
9. To encourage participants to use a switch and teach them the concept of cause and effect.
10. To have fun.

Ingredients and equipment

- Small packet cream cheese
- 1 large avocado
- 3 cloves garlic
- 1 lemon
- Black pepper
- Electric knife
- Electric juicer

- Electric food processor
- Power box
- Switches
- Chopping board
- Bowls
- Spoons

Method

1. Position group members so that they have the opportunity to greet one another, either by looking at or reaching out to each other.
2. Pass the packet of cream cheese around for participants to feel the packet and taste the cheese.
3. Pass the avocado around to feel and taste.
4. Pass the garlic around to feel, smell and taste. Using the chopping board and electric knife with power box and switch, chop the garlic.
5. Score the lemon to release the aroma, and pass around to feel and smell.
6. Cut the lemon into quarters, remove the skin, then juice the lemon using the electric juicer with power box and switch. Place participants' hands on the appliance or table to feel the vibrations.
7. Pass lemon juice around to taste.
8. Put the avocado, cream cheese and garlic in the electric food processor, and operate with power box and switch. Blend until smooth. Add black pepper to taste.
9. Sprinkle lemon juice over the dip.
10. Pass dip around to taste.
11. At the end of the activity, position group members so that they have the opportunity to say goodbye to one another, either by looking at or reaching out to each other.

CHOCOLATE PEPPERMINT SLICE

Do not use this activity if people have swallowing difficulties.

Aims

1. To provide a gustatory experience (variety of tastes).
2. To provide an olfactory experience (variety of smells).
3. To provide a tactile experience (variety of textures).
4. To provide an auditory experience (sound of the electrical equipment).
5. To encourage an interactive environment.
6. To encourage participation in the activity.
7. To provide an opportunity to express likes and dislikes.
8. To provide an opportunity to make choices.
9. To encourage participants to use a switch and teach them the concept of cause and effect.
10. To have fun.

Ingredients and equipment

- 1 packet plain tea biscuits
- 3 chocolate bars with crunchy mint pieces
- 1 small tin condensed milk
- 9 oz (250 g) dark cooking chocolate
- 2 oz (57 g) solidified coconut oil
- Dessicated coconut to decorate
- Baking tray

- Electric food processor
- Electric tin opener
- Electric frying pan
- Power box
- Switches
- Rolling pin (optional)
- Plastic bag (optional)
- Bowls

Method

1. Position group members so that they have the opportunity to greet one another, either by looking at or reaching out to each other.
2. Pass around the packet of biscuits and peppermint crisps to feel, smell and taste.
3. Using the electric food processor with power box and switch, crush the biscuits and peppermint crisps. Alternatively, crush in a plastic bag using a rolling pin, depending on participants' hand skills.
4. Using the electric tin opener with power box and switch, open the tin of condensed milk. Place participants' hands on the appliance or table to feel the vibrations.
5. Pass the milk around to smell, feel and taste.
6. Add the milk to the biscuit mixture and blend in.
7. Press the mixture into the baking tray.
8. Pass the chocolate around to smell, feel and taste.
9. Melt the chocolate and solidified coconut oil, and pour over the mixture in the baking tray. Decorate with the coconut.
10. Put the tray in the refrigerator and allow the mixture to set.
11. At the end of the activity, position group members so that they have the opportunity to say goodbye to one another, either by looking at or reaching out to each other.

CHOCOLATE SYLLABUB

Aims

1. To provide a gustatory experience (variety of tastes).
2. To provide an olfactory experience (variety of smells).
3. To provide a tactile experience (variety of textures/vibrations/temperatures).
4. To provide an auditory experience (sounds of the electrical equipment).
5. To provide an interactive environment.
6. To encourage participation in an activity.
7. To provide an opportunity to express likes and dislikes.
8. To provide an opportunity to make choices.
9. To encourage participants to use a switch and teach them the concept of cause and effect.
10. To have fun.

Ingredients and equipment

- 4 oz (125 g) plain chocolate, plus extra to decorate
- 3 tbsp brandy
- 10 fl oz (284 ml) double cream (chilled)
- 2 egg whites
- Chocolate to decorate
- Electric frying pan
- Electric whisk
- Electric grater

- Electric knife
- Electric food processor
- Power box
- Switches
- Chopping board
- Trays
- Spoons
- Small glasses/dishes
- Small lightweight jug

Method

1. Position group members so that they have the opportunity to greet one another, either by looking at or reaching out to each other.
2. Pass the packet of chocolate around to explore the wrapper.
3. Using the chopping board and electric knife with power box and switch, cut the chocolate into cubes. Pass around to smell and taste.
4. Pass the brandy around to smell and taste. Do not offer to those on medication.
5. Pass the pot of chilled cream around for participants to feel the temperature.
6. Put the chocolate into the electric food processor and blend until it is broken up. Place participants' hands on the food processor or table to feel the vibrations.
7. Put the broken chocolate and brandy in the electric frying pan and melt very gently.
8. Whisk cream using the electric whisk with the power box and switch.
9. Pass eggs around to feel.
10. Separate the eggs. Keep the whites and put the yolks on trays to pass around and feel.
11. Using the electric whisk, whisk the egg whites until they peak. Pass some around to feel.
12. Put the melted chocolate and whipped cream in the electric food processor and mix.
13. Add the egg whites and fold in.
14. Grate some chocolate using the electric grater with power box and switch.
15. Pour the syllabub mix into the jug and co-actively pour into individual glasses/dishes.
16. Sprinkle the grated chocolate on top and enjoy!
17. At the end of the activity, position group members so that they have the opportunity to say goodbye to one another, either by looking at or reaching out to each other.

CHRISTMAS TREE SHORTBREADS

Aims

1. To provide a gustatory experience (variety of tastes).
2. To provide an olfactory experience (variety of smells).
3. To provide a tactile experience (different textures).
4. To provide an auditory experience (sound of the electrical equipment, chocolate wrappers, silver foil).
5. To provide a visual experience (looking at the silver foil, coloured tissue paper).
6. To encourage an interactive environment.
7. To encourage participation in the activity.
8. To provide an opportunity to express likes and dislikes.
9. To provide an opportunity to make choices.
10. To encourage participants to use a switch and teach them the concept of cause and effect.
11. To have fun.

Ingredients and equipment

- 2 cups plain flour
- 2 tbsp rice flour
- ⅓ cup icing sugar
- 9 oz (250 g) butter
- To add different tastes choose from the following:
  - peppermint essence
  - almond essence
  - orange rind (very finely grated)
  - desiccated coconut (check with a speech pathologist whether or not people can eat this)
  - chocolate
- Silver balls

- Icing pen (these have a small spout which allows you to draw thin lines/write with them)
- Electric food processor
- Power box
- Switches
- Rolling pin (optional)
- Bowls
- Cling film
- Christmas tree-shaped cutter
- Baking tray with baking paper or oil spray
- Skewer
- Glittery ribbon
- Wire cooling rack

Method

1. Position group members so that they have the opportunity to greet one another, either by looking at or reaching out to each other.
2. Plug the electric food processor into the power box and attach the switch.
3. Put flours and icing sugar into the food processor and mix using the switch. Place participants' hands on the appliance or table to feel the vibrations.
4. Add butter to the food processor and mix using the switch.
5. If there is time, wrap the dough in cling film and leave to chill in the fridge for 20 minutes.
6. While the shortbread dough is chilling, pass the ingredients around to smell, taste and feel. Assist participants to feel and look at the ribbon as well.
7. Bang the dough out on the table to flatten it, using hands or a rolling pin.
8. Use the Christmas tree-shaped cutter to cut out shapes from the dough. Use an adapted cutter by adding vertical or T bar handles.

9. Use the skewer to make a hole in the top of each tree shape (support people may need to do this if group members lack fine motor skills).

10. Place on baking tray and put in the oven at 160°C (315°F) for 10–15 minutes.

11. While cooking, clean up.

12. When cooked, leave to stand for 5 minutes so that the shortbreads become firm then place them on a wire rack to cool completely.

13. Decorate by piping icing around the edges and adding the silver balls and ribbon (support people may need to decorate the shortbreads if group members lack fine motor skills).

14. At the end of the activity, position group members so that they have the opportunity to say goodbye to one another, either by looking at or reaching out to each other.

CURRY PASTE

Aims

1. To provide a gustatory experience (variety of tastes).
2. To provide an olfactory experience (variety of smells).
3. To provide a tactile experience (variety of textures).
4. To provide an auditory experience (sounds of the electrical equipment).
5. To encourage an interactive environment.
6. To encourage participation in the activity.
7. To provide an opportunity to express likes and dislikes.
8. To provide an opportunity to make choices.
9. To encourage participants to use a switch and teach them the concept of cause and effect.
10. To have fun.

Ingredients and equipment

- 1 tsp ground cinnamon
- 6 red chillies, stems removed
- 6 cloves garlic
- 2 onions
- 2 cm cube fresh ginger
- 2 stalks lemon grass or rind of ½ lemon
- 1 tbsp ground coriander
- 1 tbsp ground cumin
- ¼ tsp ground cloves
- ¼ tsp ground cardamom
- ¼ tsp ground black pepper
- Electric knife
- Electric frying pan

- Electric grinder
- Electric grater
- Electric food processor
- Power box
- Switches
- Chopping board
- Bowls
- Spoons
- Jars with lids
- Decorations (different types of ribbon)
- White labels
- UV lamp

Method

1. Position group members so that they have the opportunity to greet one another, either by looking at or reaching out to each other.
2. Pass the chillies, garlic, onion, ginger and lemon grass/lemon around to smell and feel. Ensure that participants do not rub their eyes after feeling the chillies.
3. Using the chopping board and the electric knife with power box and switch, chop the ginger and quarter the onions. Place participants' hands on the appliance or table to feel the vibrations. Pass some of the ginger and onions around to taste.
4. Place the chillies, garlic, onions, ginger and lemon grass in the electric food processor and blend.
5. If using a lemon instead of the lemon grass, score the skin to release the aroma, and pass around to smell and feel. Use the electric grater to grate the rind and pass some of the lemon around to taste.
6. Pass around all the remaining spices to smell, taste and feel.
7. If there is time, grind the spices in an electric grinder rather than buying ready-ground spices.

8. Place all remaining spices in the electric frying pan and stir over a low heat for 2–3 minutes. Encourage participants to enjoy the aroma of the roasted spices.

9. Remove from heat, cool slightly and add to the electric food processor with the other ingredients.

10. Blend the ingredients until smooth. Pass the paste around to smell and taste.

11. Pass the ribbons around to feel and look at.

12. Look at the white labels under a UV lamp.

13. Put the paste into small jars and decorate. Store in a refrigerator.

14. At the end of the activity, position group members so that they have the opportunity to say goodbye to one another, either by looking at or reaching out to each other.

DECORATING A PLAIN CAKE

Aims

1. To provide a gustatory experience (variety of tastes).
2. To provide an olfactory experience (variety of smells).
3. To provide a tactile experience (different textures).
4. To encourage an interactive environment.
5. To encourage participation in the activity.
6. To provide an opportunity to express likes and dislikes.
7. To provide an opportunity to make choices.
8. To have fun.

Ingredients and equipment

- Plain cake
- Food colouring
- Icing sugar
- Rosewater
- Angelica
- Mint leaves
- Silver balls
- Hundreds and thousands

- Chocolate sprinkles
- Glacé cherries
- Large plate
- Bowls
- Spoons
- Knife
- Small jug

Method

1. Position group members so that they have the opportunity to greet one another, either by looking at or reaching out to each other.
2. Place the plain cake on a large plate.
3. Place the different decorations in bowls and pass around to feel, smell and taste. Liaise with a speech pathologist as some individuals may not be able to eat some of the decorations (e.g. silver balls).
4. Using the small jug, co-actively pour the icing sugar into a bowl to feel and taste.
5. Divide the icing sugar into smaller bowls and add different food colourings. Note whether or not participants have a particular colour preference.
6. Pass the rosewater around to smell and taste; add it to the icing sugar if group members indicate that they like it.
7. Put icing on the cake and add the various decorations.
8. Encourage participants to choose what they want to put on the cake and where to put it. Alternatively, make individual fairy cakes so that they can decorate their own cakes.
9. At the end of the activity, position group members so that they have the opportunity to say goodbye to one another, either by looking at or reaching out to each other.

FROZEN APPLE

Note that time needs to be allowed for the mixture to freeze.

Aims

1. To provide a gustatory experience (variety of tastes).
2. To provide an olfactory experience (variety of smells).
3. To provide a tactile experience (variety of textures/temperatures).
4. To provide an auditory experience (sounds of the electrical equipment).
5. To encourage an interactive environment.
6. To encourage participation in the activity.
7. To provide an opportunity to express likes and dislikes.
8. To provide an opportunity to make choices.
9. To encourage participants to use a switch and teach them the concept of cause and effect.
10. To have fun.

Ingredients and equipment

- ¼ cup sugar
- ½ cup water
- 1 tbsp brandy
- 2 cups (500 ml) unsweetened apple juice
- 2 tbsp fresh mint
- 1 egg white
  Variation
- Oranges (enough for 2 cups juice)
- Grapefruit (enough for ½ cup juice)
- Electric food processor/blender
- Electric juicer

- Electric knife
- Electric frying pan
- Power box
- Switches
- Chopping board
- Plastic bag
- Ice cube tray
- Aluminium foil
- Bowls
- Spoons

Method

1. Position group members so that they have the opportunity to greet one another, either by looking at or reaching out to each other.
2. Pour sugar into a bowl to feel and taste.
3. Offer participants a smell and taste of the brandy, unless they are on medication.
4. Combine sugar, water and brandy in the electric frying pan (connected to the power box and switch) and ask someone to turn it on with their switch.
5. Cook over a medium heat and stir until the sugar dissolves.
6. Bring to the boil, then reduce heat and simmer, without stirring, for 5 minutes until the mixture thickens. Allow to cool to room temperature.
7. While the mixture is thickening and cooling, take the apple juice and offer it to participants to smell and taste.
8. Pass around the mint to smell and feel.
9. Use the chopping board and electric knife or food processor, with the power box and switch, to finely chop the mint.

10. Place the apple juice, mint and cooled sugar syrup in the food processor/blender and mix together. Place participants' hands on the appliance or table to feel the vibrations.

11. Pass the mixture around to taste.

12. Pour the mixture into the ice cube tray, cover with aluminium foil and freeze until set.

13. Offer participants some aluminium foil to explore and feel.

14. Beat the egg white in the electric blender/food processor, with power box and switch, until stiff peaks form.

15. Offer participants some of the mixture to feel.

16. Remove the frozen mixture from the ice cube tray and put some in a plastic bag. Offer participants the bag to feel.

17. Use the electric blender/food processor, with power box and switch, to break up the frozen mixture.

18. Fold in the egg white.

19. Offer participants the mixture to taste.

20. At the end of the activity, position group members so that they have the opportunity to say goodbye to one other, either by looking at or reaching out to each other.

As a variation, use orange and grapefruit juice (extracted from the fruit using the electric juicer) instead of the apple and mint.

FRUIT CHEESE ROLL

Do not do this activity with participants that have eating difficulties.

Aims

1. To provide a gustatory experience (variety of tastes).
2. To provide an olfactory experience (variety of smells).
3. To provide a tactile experience (variety of textures/vibrations).
4. To provide an auditory experience (sounds of the electrical equipment).
5. To encourage an interactive environment.
6. To encourage participation in the activity.
7. To provide an opportunity to express likes and dislikes.
8. To provide an opportunity to make choices.
9. To encourage participants to use a switch and teach them the concept of cause and effect.
10. To have fun.

Ingredients and equipment

- 9 oz (250 g) cream cheese
- ¼ cup sultanas
- ½ cup chopped dried apricots
- ½ cup tasty cheese
- 1 tbsp mixed peel
- 2 tbsp sweet sherry
- 1 lemon (1 tsp grated lemon rind for recipe)
- ¾ cup poppy seeds

- Electric food processor
- Electric knife
- Electric grater
- Power box
- Switches
- Chopping board
- Bowls
- Spoons

Method

1. Position group members so that they have the opportunity to greet one another, either by looking at or reaching out to each other.
2. Score the lemon to release the aroma, and pass around to smell and feel.
3. Using the chopping board and electric knife with power box and switch, cut the rind off the lemon. Cut this into small pieces.
4. Using the electric grater with power box and switch, grate the tasty cheese and pass around to taste.
5. Using the electric food processor with power box and switch, beat the cream cheese and tasty cheese until smooth. Place the participants' hands on the processor or table to feel the vibrations.
6. Co-actively assist participants to pour in the lemon rind, mixed peel, sherry and fruit and mix with the cheeses.
7. Refrigerate until firm.
8. While the mix is in the refrigerator, pass around all the other ingredients to smell, taste and feel.
9. Roll the mixture into a log or small balls. Pour poppy seeds onto a tray or bowl and roll the log in the poppy seeds.
10. Cover and store in the refrigerator for up to 4 days.
11. At the end of the activity, position group members so that they have the opportunity to say goodbye to one another, either by looking at or reaching out to each other.

FUDGE

The fudge can be made during one activity and the baskets during another.

Aims

1. To provide a gustatory experience (variety of tastes).
2. To provide an olfactory experience (variety of smells).
3. To provide a tactile experience (variety of textures).
4. To provide an auditory experience (sound of the electrical equipment, chocolate wrappers, silver foil).
5. To provide a visual experience (looking at the silver foil, coloured tissue paper).
6. To encourage an interactive environment.
7. To encourage participation in the activity.
8. To provide an opportunity to express likes and dislikes.
9. To provide an opportunity to make choices.
10. To encourage participants to use a switch and teach them the concept of cause and effect.
11. To have fun.

Ingredients and equipment

- 9 oz (250 g) dark chocolate
- 9 oz (250 g) milk chocolate
- 1 small tin condensed milk
- 2 oz (60 g) butter
- Peppermint essence
- Vanilla essence
- Orange essence or Cointreau
- Sultanas
- Electric knife
- Electric tin opener
- Power box
- Switches
- Chopping board
- Microwave-proof bowl
- Microwave
- Baking trays
- Silver foil
- Spoons
- Bowls
- Small wire baskets
- Greaseproof paper
- Coloured tissue paper
- 'Made by' stamp, adapted with large handle
- White labels
- UV lamp
- Ribbon (coloured, silver/gold, glittery)

Method

Activity 1: fudge

1. Position group members so that they have the opportunity to greet one another, either by looking at or reaching out to each other.
2. Pass chocolate around in the packet for them to feel and listen to by scrunching the packet.
3. With the power box and switch, use the electric knife and chopping board to cut the chocolate into small blocks. Place participants' hands on the appliance or table to feel the vibrations.
4. With the power box and switch, use the electric tin opener to open the tin of condensed milk.
5. Pass condensed milk around to smell and taste.

6.   Pass essences around to smell.

7.   Pass Cointreau around to smell and taste. Do not offer to participants on medication.

8.   Put the chocolate, milk and butter in the microwave-proof bowl and melt in the microwave for about 3 minutes. Adjust this time depending on the microwave: if the chocolate is overheated, it will go hard and lumpy. As a variation, leave out the chocolate and add vanilla and sultanas. Do not use sultanas if people have eating difficulties.

9.   Divide the fudge mix into three: put peppermint essence in one batch, vanilla in another and orange essence or Cointreau in the third.

10.   Pass the fudge mixes around to taste.

11.   Line baking trays with silver foil and put the fudge into tins. Put in the fridge to set.

12.   Pass some silver foil round for participants to explore.

13.   At the end of the activity, position group members so that they have the opportunity to say goodbye to one another, either by looking at or reaching out to each other.

Activity 2: baskets

1.   Position group members so that they can greet one another, either by looking at or reaching out to each other.

2.   Pass silver foil, coloured tissue paper and greaseproof paper around to look at and feel.

3.   Look at the white labels under the UV lamp.

4.   Use the 'made by' stamp on the labels and write the list of ingredients on the labels.

5.   Pass ribbon around to look at and feel.

6.   Pass baskets around to look at and feel.

7.   Decorate baskets with the ribbon and stick a label on the base of the basket.

8.   When the fudge has set, peel it away from the silver foil and cut the fudge into small squares.

9.   Pass fudge around to taste. Note if individuals have a preference for the different fudges.

10.   Place tissue paper in a basket and line the bottom with greaseproof paper. Put fudge on the greaseproof paper. Repeat with other baskets and give as gifts.

11.   At the end of the activity, position group members so that they have the opportunity to say goodbye to one another, either by looking at or reaching out to each other.

GRAPEFRUIT SORBET

Note that this needs time to freeze.

Aims

1. To provide a gustatory experience (variety of tastes).
2. To provide an olfactory experience (variety of smells).
3. To provide a tactile experience (variety of textures/temperatures).
4. To provide an auditory experience (sounds of the electrical equipment).
5. To encourage an interactive environment.
6. To encourage participation in the activity.
7. To provide an opportunity to express likes and dislikes.
8. To provide an opportunity to make choices.
9. To encourage participants to use a switch and teach them the concept of cause and effect.
10. To have fun.

Ingredients and equipment

- 1 oz (28 g) honey
- ½ pint (300 ml) water
- 2 cans (450 g) grapefruit segments in natural juice
- ¼ pint (150 ml) lemon juice
- Grated rind of 2 lemons
- 2 egg whites
- Sprigs of mint for decoration
- Electric can opener

- Electric juicer
- Electric grater
- Electric frying pan
- Electric whisk
- Power box
- Switches
- Strainer
- Bowls
- Spoons

Method

1. Position group members so that they have the opportunity to greet one another, either by looking at or reaching out to each other.
2. Use the electric can opener with power box and switch to open the cans of grapefruit.
3. Pass the grapefruit around to smell and taste the segments and juice.
4. Score the lemons to release the aroma, and pass around for group members to feel and smell.
5. Using the electric juicer with power box and switch, squeeze the lemons. Pass juice around to taste.
6. Using the electric grater with power box and switch, grate the lemon rind. Place participants' hands on the appliance or table to feel the vibrations.
7. Pour honey into bowls and pass around to feel, smell and taste.
8. Pass mint around to feel, taste and smell.
9. Pass eggs around to feel. Separate the yolks from the whites and pass the yolks around to feel.
10. Place honey and water together in the electric frying pan and gently bring to the boil. Simmer for 5 minutes.
11. Turn off the heat and cool slightly.
12. Drain the grapefruit juice from one of the cans of segments.

13. Using the electric whisk, with power box and switch, mix the grapefruit juice, honey liquid, lemon juice and lemon rind.

14. Place in the freezer until half-frozen.

15. Whisk the egg whites until stiff, then fold into the mixture.

16. Freeze again until firm.

17. Serve the sorbet on a bed of grapefruit segments and top with mint sprigs.

18. At the end of the activity, position group members so that they have the opportunity to say goodbye to one other, either by looking at or reaching out to each other.

HUMMUS

Aims

1. To provide an olfactory experience (variety of smells).
2. To provide a gustatory experience (variety of tastes).
3. To provide a tactile experience (variety of textures/vibrations).
4. To provide an auditory experience (sounds of the electrical equipment).
5. To encourage an interactive environment.
6. To encourage participation in the activity.
7. To provide an opportunity to express likes and dislikes.
8. To encourage participants to use a switch and teach them the concept of cause and effect.
9. To have fun.

Ingredients and equipment

- 15 oz (425 g) can chickpeas
- Garlic cloves (1 garlic clove, peeled and crushed, for recipe)
- 1 tbsp olive oil
- 2 tsp tahini
- 1 lemon (2–3 tsp lemon juice for recipe)
- Salt and pepper
- Paprika
- Power box
- Switches
- Electric can opener
- Electric knife
- Electric juicer
- Electric food processor/blender
- Chopping board
- Spoons
- Small jars with lids
- Labels
- UV lamp
- 'Made by' stamp, adapted with large handle

Method

1. Position group members so that they have the opportunity to greet one another, either by looking at or reaching out to each other.
2. Use the electric can opener with power box and switch to open the can of chickpeas.
3. Drain the chickpeas (reserve the liquid), put some in a bowl to pass around and feel, and put the rest in the electric food processor/blender.
4. Add enough of the chickpea liquid to make a thick, creamy purée and blend using the power box and switch.
5. Pass garlic around to smell and taste. Add 1 crushed garlic clove to the chickpea mixture and blend.
6. Pass tahini around to smell and taste. Add 2 teaspoons of tahini to the chickpea mixture, then 1 tablespoon of olive oil, and blend.
7. Pass lemon around to smell and feel. Score the lemon first to release the aroma.
8. Using the chopping board and electric knife with power box and switch, cut the lemon in half, and pass around to smell.
9. Use the electric juicer to squeeze the lemon. Place participants' hands on the juicer or table to feel the vibrations.
10. Pass lemon juice around to taste; add 2–3 teaspoons of it to sharpen the mixture and then blend.

11. Add salt and pepper to taste and blend.

12. Pass paprika around to smell and taste. Sprinkle on top of the hummus.

13. Pass some hummus around to taste and place the rest in jars for gifts.

14. Look at the white labels under the UV lamp.

15. Write the ingredients on labels, use the 'made by' stamp and then stick the labels onto the jars.

16. At the end of the activity, position group members so that they have the opportunity to say goodbye to one another, either by looking at or reaching out to each other.

INDIAN SAMOSA FILLING

Aims

1. To provide a gustatory experience (variety of tastes).
2. To provide an olfactory experience (variety of smells).
3. To provide a tactile experience (variety of textures).
4. To provide an auditory experience (sound of the electrical equipment).
5. To encourage an interactive environment.
6. To encourage participation in the activity.
7. To provide an opportunity to express likes and dislikes.
8. To provide an opportunity to make choices.
9. To encourage participants to use a switch and teach them the concept of cause and effect.
10. To have fun.

Ingredients and equipment

The following quantities make 36 samosas. Reduce if you are working with a small group.

- 1 tbsp oil
- 1 lb (500 g) minced steak or lamb
- 2 in (5 cm) piece green ginger
- 2 cloves garlic
- 1 large onion
- Salt and pepper
- 1 tsp garam masala
- ½ tsp turmeric
- ¼ tsp chilli powder
- 1 cup water

- Power box
- Switches
- Chopping board
- Electric knife
- Electric food processor
- Electric frying pan
- Small jug
- Bowls
- Teaspoons
- Wooden spoon

Method

1. Position group members so that they have the opportunity to greet one another, either by looking at or reaching out to each other.
2. Pass around ginger to feel, taste and smell.
3. Pass around garlic to feel, taste and smell.
4. Pass around onion to feel and smell.
5. Pass around garam masala, turmeric and chilli powder to smell and taste (in very small quantities).
6. Pass around salt and pepper to smell and taste.
7. Peel the ginger and grate/chop finely using the electric food processor with power box and switch. Place participants' hands on the appliance or table to feel the vibrations.
8. Peel the garlic and chop finely using either the chopping board and electric knife or the electric food processor, with the power box and switch.
9. Use the electric knife to cut the onion into quarters.
10. Chop the onion finely using the electric food processor with power box and switch. Pass around to smell and taste.
11. Heat oil in the electric frying pan, add the meat and stir with the wooden spoon until the meat is light golden brown. Add the ginger, garlic, onion, spices and seasoning.

12. Using a small jug, co-actively assist a participant to pour water into the frying pan and stir into the mixture.

13. Bring the mixture to the boil, reduce the heat and set aside to simmer, uncovered, for 25–30 minutes, or until nearly all the liquid has evaporated. Clean up while the meat is cooking.

14. Offer participants a taste of the mixture and note their reactions.

15. As an alternative to the above sequence, make up the mixture and, while it is cooking, offer participants the opportunity to smell, taste and feel extra portions of the individual ingredients.

16. At the end of the activity, position group members so that they have the opportunity to say goodbye to one another, either by looking at or reaching out to each other.

LEMON AND PASSIONFRUIT CREAM

If any participants have swallowing difficulties, use apple and pear instead.

Aims

1. To provide a gustatory experience (variety of tastes).
2. To provide an olfactory experience (variety of smells).
3. To provide a tactile experience (variety of textures).
4. To provide an auditory experience (sound of the electrical equipment).
5. To encourage an interactive environment.
6. To encourage participation in the activity.
7. To provide an opportunity to express likes and dislikes.
8. To provide an opportunity to make choices.
9. To encourage participants to use a switch and teach them the concept of cause and effect.
10. To have fun.

Ingredients and equipment

- 2 × 1¼ oz (35 g) sachets sugar-free lemon jelly crystals
- ½ cup (125 ml) boiling water
- 3 tbsp cold water
- 1 cup (250 ml) evaporated skimmed milk (chilled)
- Pulp of 2 passionfruits
- Lemon rind strips and passionfruit pulp for garnish

- Electric food mixer
- Electric knife
- Electric tin opener
- Power box
- Switches
- Chopping board
- Spoons
- Dessert bowls/glasses

Method

1. Position group members so that they have the opportunity to greet one another, either by looking at or reaching out to each other.
2. Open one of the sachets of jelly crystals and encourage participants to feel, smell and taste the crystals.
3. Use the food mixer with power box and switch to mix the second sachet of jelly crystals with boiling water. Place participants' hands on the appliance or table to feel the vibrations. Mix until crystals have dissolved.
4. Blend in the cold water using the electric food mixer and set aside.
5. Open the tin of skimmed milk with the electric tin opener plugged into the power box and switch.
6. Offer participants a taste of the skimmed milk.
7. Beat the skimmed milk in the food mixer until thick.
8. Pass around a passionfruit for participants to smell and feel.
9. Use the chopping board and electric knife with power box and switch to cut open the passionfruit.
10. Offer participants a taste of the passionfruit. Do not do this if individuals have swallowing difficulties.

11. Using a spoon, scoop out the passionfruit pulp and mix together with the dissolved crystals.

12. Spoon the mixture into dessert bowls/glasses and chill until set.

13. Pass around lemon to feel and smell. Score the lemon first, to release the aroma.

14. Using the chopping board and electric knife with the power box and switch, cut open the lemon and cut strips of lemon rind.

15. Offer participants a taste and smell of the lemon.

16. Just before serving, top with lemon rind and passionfruit pulp.

17. At the end of the activity, position group members so that they have the opportunity to say goodbye to one another, either by looking at or reaching out to each other.

MAKING LUNCH: CRUSTLESS QUICHE

Aims

1. To provide a gustatory experience (variety of tastes).
2. To provide an olfactory experience (variety of smells).
3. To provide a tactile experience (variety of textures).
4. To provide an auditory experience (sound of the electrical equipment).
5. To encourage group members to participate in making their own lunch.
6. To encourage an interactive environment.
7. To provide an opportunity for participants to taste, smell and feel the different ingredients used in the lunch preparation.
8. To provide an opportunity to express likes and dislikes.
9. To provide an opportunity for participants to use a switch and teach them the concept of cause and effect.
10. To have fun.

Ingredients and equipment

- 1½ cups cheddar cheese
- ¾ cup corn kernels (tinned)
- 10 mushrooms
- 3 spring onions
- 3 courgettes
- 3 tomatoes
- 6 eggs
- 1 cup milk
- Electric food processor/blender

- Electric tin opener
- Electric knife
- Power box
- Switches
- Microwave-proof dish
- Microwave
- Chopping board
- Paper towels
- Jug

Method

1. Position group members so that they have the opportunity to greet one another, either by looking at or reaching out to each other.
2. Throughout the activity, offer participants the opportunity to feel, taste and smell the different ingredients.
3. Wipe the courgettes and, using the chopping board and electric knife with power box and switch, cut them into cubes.
4. Put the cubes in the electric food processor and, using the grater tool and the power box and switch, grate the courgettes. Place participants' hands on the appliance or table to feel the vibrations.
5. Assist participants to remove any moisture with paper towels.
6. Use the chopping board and electric knife to chop the tomatoes, mushrooms and spring onions.
7. Open the tin of corn kernels using the electric tin opener with power box and switch.
8. Chop the cheese into cubes using the chopping board and electric knife, then grate these in the food processor.
9. Assist participants to put vegetables into the microwave-proof dish then add the cheese.
10. Whisk the eggs and milk in the electric blender using the power box and switch.
11. Assist participants to pour the eggs and milk over the vegetables and cheese.

12. Cook for 5 minutes in the microwave on medium power. Adjust the time depending on the microwave you are using.
13. Assist participants to help with cleaning up (e.g. drying dishes and wiping down the table).
14. Eat lunch.
15. At the end of the activity, position group members so that they have the opportunity to say goodbye to one another, either by looking at or reaching out to each other.

PANCAKES

Aims

1. To provide an olfactory experience (variety of smells).
2. To provide a gustatory experience (variety of tastes).
3. To provide a tactile experience (variety of textures).
4. To provide an auditory experience (sound of the electrical equipment).
5. To provide a visual experience (tracking the ingredients).
6. To encourage an interactive environment.
7. To encourage participation in the activity.
8. To provide an opportunity to express likes and dislikes.
9. To provide an opportunity to make choices.
10. To encourage participants to use a switch and teach them the concept of cause and effect.
11. To have fun.

Ingredients and equipment

- 1 tbsp butter
- 2 eggs (1 for feeling)
- ¾ cup milk
- ½ cup flour (plus extra to feel)
- Different jams
- Maple syrup
- Cream
- Fruit (e.g. bananas)
- Sugar
- Lemon
- Electric blender
- Electric frying pan
- Electric beater
- Electric knife
- Electric juicer
- Power box
- Switches
- Fish slice
- Spoons
- Small jug
- Tray
- Bowls
- Sieve
- Measuring cups

Method

1. Position group members so that they have the opportunity to greet one another, either by looking at or reaching out to each other.
2. Co-actively assist a participant to pour the flour into a bowl and pass the bowl of flour around for everyone to feel.
3. Measure out ½ cup of flour and put in the jug. Co-actively assist a participant to pour the flour into the sieve. Sieve the flour over a bowl then pour into the electric blender. Place participants' hands on the appliance or table to feel the vibrations. Encourage participants to track the flour as it moves through the sieve into the bowl.
4. Put 1 egg on a tray and pass it around to feel. Break the egg; allow participants to feel the difference and watch how it slides around the tray.
5. Add the other egg to the blender.
6. Measure out ¾ cup of milk and put in the jug. Co-actively assist a participant to pour the milk into the blender.
7. Measure out 1 tablespoon of butter. Co-actively assist a participant to put the butter in the electric frying pan.

8. Using the power box and switch, turn on the electric frying pan and melt the butter. Encourage participants to smell the melted butter and listen to it sizzling.

9. Pour the melted butter into the jug and co-actively assist a participant to pour the butter into the blender.

10. Using the blender with the power box and switch, get participants to take it in turns to beat the pancake mix.

11. Use the jug to pour a small amount of the mixture into the frying pan to cook.

12. While the pancakes are cooking, pass around the jams, maple syrup and fruit for participants to taste.

13. Score the lemon to release the aroma, and pass around to feel and smell.

14. Using the chopping board and electric knife with power box and switch, cut up the chosen fruit and cut the lemon into quarters, removing the rind.

15. Use the electric juicer with power box and switch to extract the lemon juice.

16. Pass lemon juice around to smell and taste.

17. Using the electric beater with power box and switch, whip up the cream.

18. Using the fish slice, remove the pancakes from the frying pan.

19. Offer participants the choice of maple syrup, jams, sugar, lemon, fruit and cream to eat with their pancakes.

20. At the end of the activity, position group members so that they have the opportunity to say goodbye to one another, either by looking at or reaching out to each other.

RITA'S SPONGE FINGER CAKE

Aims

1. To provide a gustatory experience (variety of tastes).
2. To provide an olfactory experience (variety of smells).
3. To provide a tactile experience (variety of textures).
4. To provide an auditory experience (sound of the electrical equipment).
5. To encourage an interactive environment.
6. To encourage participation in the activity.
7. To provide an opportunity to express likes and dislikes.
8. To provide an opportunity to make choices.
9. To encourage participants to use a switch and teach them the concept of cause and effect.
10. To have fun.

Ingredients and equipment

- 1 packet sponge finger biscuits
- 2 cartons long-life cream
- 7 oz (200 g) ricotta cheese
- Roasted hazelnuts/walnuts
- 1 small bar chocolate
- 1 lemon
- ½ cup strong coffee
- ½ cup Marsala wine
- Electric food processor/grinder
- Electric whisk
- Electric knife
- Electric grater
- Power box
- Switches
- Chopping board
- Rectangular dish
- Small bowls
- Spoons
- Spatula
- Shallow dish
- Small jug

Method

1. Position group members so that they have the opportunity to greet one another, either by looking at or reaching out to each other.
2. Pass around strong coffee to smell and taste.
3. Pass around Marsala to smell and taste. Do not offer to people on medication.
4. Whip the cream using the electric whisk with power box and switch. Place participants' hands on the appliance or table to feel the vibrations.
5. Score the lemon to release the aroma, and pass around to smell and feel.
6. Using the chopping board and electric knife with power box and switch, cut the rind off the lemon.
7. Grate the lemon rind using the electric grater with power box and switch. Keep most of the rind and pass the remainder around to smell and feel.
8. Pass around nuts to taste and smell, then grind up finely in the food processor/grinder. Omit the nuts from the recipe if any individuals have eating difficulties.
9. Pass around the chocolate to feel and taste.
10. Grate the chocolate using the electric grater with power box and switch, then pass around to taste.
11. Pass around ricotta cheese to taste.

12. Pass around the packet of sponge fingers to feel and listen to the noise the packet makes when scrunched or shaken.

13. Using the small jug, co-actively assist participants to pour the Marsala and coffee into a shallow dish.

14. Open the packet of biscuits and co-actively assist participants to lay the biscuits in the dish. Remove the biscuits as soon as they have soaked up the liquid. If left in too long, they will start to fall apart.

15. Co-actively assist participants to lay the biscuits along the bottom of the rectangular dish.

16. Co-actively assist participants, using the spatula, to put a layer of cream and cheese on top of the biscuits and then sprinkle on the nuts, lemon rind and grated chocolate.

17. Co-actively assist participants to repeat the layers and decorate the top with the grated nuts and chocolate.

18. Pass around finished cake to taste and note participants' reactions.

19. At the end of the activity, position group members so that they have the opportunity to say goodbye to one another, either by looking at or reaching out to each other.

SMALL CHRISTMAS PUDDINGS

The puddings can be made during one activity, the baskets during another.

Aims

1. To provide a gustatory experience (variety of tastes).
2. To provide an olfactory experience (variety of smells).
3. To provide a tactile experience (variety of textures/vibrations).
4. To provide an auditory experience (sounds of the electrical equipment, chocolate wrappers).
5. To provide a visual experience (looking at the coloured tissue paper).
6. To encourage an interactive environment.
7. To encourage participation in the activity.
8. To provide an opportunity to express likes and dislikes.
9. To provide an opportunity to make choices.
10. To encourage participants to use a switch and teach them the concept of cause and effect.
11. To have fun.

Ingredients and equipment

- 1 dark Christmas cake
- 9 oz (250 g) white chocolate
- 2 oranges
- Glacé cherries
- Electric knife
- Electric food processor
- Electric juicer
- Power box
- Switches
- Spoons
- Glass bowl
- Bowls
- Chopping board

- Microwave (or double boiler)
- Flat board/tins
- Small wire baskets
- Silver foil
- Greaseproof paper
- Coloured tissue paper
- 'Made by' stamp, adapted with large handle
- White labels
- UV lamp
- Ribbon (coloured, silver/ gold, glittery)

Method

Activity 1: puddings

1. Position group members so that they have the opportunity to greet one another, either by looking at or reaching out to each other.
2. Pass cake around in wrapper to feel and listen to.
3. Use the chopping board and electric knife with power box and switch to cut cake into blocks.
4. Pass cake around to smell and taste, unless any participants have eating difficulties.
5. Score an orange to release the aroma, and pass around to smell and feel.
6. Cut oranges in half or pieces and juice in the electric juicer. Encourage participants to place their hands on the juicer or table to feel the vibrations.
7. Pass orange juice around to smell and taste.

8. Put cake and a small amount of orange juice into the electric food processor. Keep some cake aside in case you put in too much juice. The cake and juice should become a soft ball that you can mould.

9. Pass around some of the mixture to taste.

10. Roll small pieces of cake into balls and put onto the board or tray.

11. Pass the chocolate around in the packet to feel and listen to by scrunching the packet.

12. Use the chopping board and electric knife with power box and switch to cut chocolate into small blocks.

13. Put the chocolate in the glass bowl and melt in the microwave or double boiler.

14. Pass the packet of cherries around to feel.

15. Cut the cherries into small pieces using the chopping board and electric knife, and pass around to taste and smell, unless any participants have eating difficulties.

16. When the chocolate has melted, put blobs of chocolate on the top of the cakes. Keep aside some to taste.

17. Immediately put pieces of cherry on top before the chocolate hardens.

18. The chocolate will harden quickly so finish decorating the cakes before passing around to smell and taste.

19. Put in the fridge to set.

20. At the end of the activity, position group members so that they have the opportunity to say goodbye to one another, either by looking at or reaching out to each other.

Activity 2: baskets

1. Position group members so that they have the opportunity to greet one another, either by looking at or reaching out to each other.

2. Pass the silver foil, coloured tissue paper and greaseproof paper around to look at and feel.

3. Look at the white labels under the UV lamp.

4. Use the 'made by' stamp on the labels and add a list of ingredients.

5. Pass ribbon around to look at and feel.

6. Pass baskets around to look at and feel.

7. Decorate the baskets with the ribbon.

8. Pass cakes around to taste.

9. Place tissue paper in each basket and line the bottom with greaseproof paper. Put the cakes on the greaseproof paper and give as gifts.

10. At the end of the activity, position group members so that they have the opportunity to say goodbye to one another, either by looking at or reaching out to each other.

STRAWBERRY AND PEACH COBBLER

Aims

1. To provide a gustatory experience (variety of tastes).
2. To provide an olfactory experience (variety of smells).
3. To provide a tactile experience (variety of textures).
4. To provide an auditory experience (sound of the electrical equipment).
5. To encourage an interactive environment.
6. To encourage participation in the activity.
7. To provide an opportunity to express likes and dislikes.
8. To provide an opportunity to make choices.
9. To encourage participants to use a switch and teach them the concept of cause and effect.
10. To have fun.

Ingredients and equipment

- 1 punnet strawberries
- 1 small tin sliced peaches
- 2 tbsp sugar
- 1 tbsp butter
  For the dumplings
- 1 cup self-raising flour
- 1 tbsp butter
- 2 tbsp milk powder
- $\frac{1}{3}$ cup water
- 1 egg
- $\frac{1}{2}$ tsp cinnamon

- Microwave-proof dish
- Microwave
- Electric tin opener
- Power box
- Switches
- Electric knife
- Electric food processor
- Chopping board
- Spoons
- Bowls

Method

1. Position group members so that they have the opportunity to greet one another, either by looking at or reaching out to each other.
2. Use the electric tin opener with power box and switch to open the tin of peaches.
3. Offer participants a taste of the peach and peach juice.
4. Wash the strawberries and use the chopping board and electric knife with power box and switch to cut them into halves. Offer participants a taste of the strawberries.
5. Place strawberries and peaches with juice in a microwave dish. Heat uncovered on high power for 5 minutes. Adjust timing according to the microwave. Remove.
6. Place all the dumpling ingredients in the electric food processor and use power box and switches to mix. Place participants' hands on the appliance or table to feel the vibrations.
7. Offer participants a taste of the milk powder.
8. Offer participants a smell and taste of cinnamon.
9. Remove the peaches from the dish and place the strawberries in juice in the electric food processor to crush. Remember to move the food processor so that it is in front of participants when it is their turn to use the switch.
10. Place the peaches and crushed strawberries in juice back in the microwave dish. Add spoonfuls of dumpling mix like 'islands' in the fruit mixture.
11. Cook on high power, covered, for 5 minutes.

12.   Remove from the microwave and leave to cool.

13.   Offer participants a taste of the finished product and note their reactions.

14.   At the end of the activity, position group members so that they have the opportunity to say goodbye to one another, either by looking at or reaching out to each other.

SUMMER PUDDING

Make this during one activity and serve it the next day.

Aims

1. To provide a gustatory experience (variety of tastes).
2. To provide an olfactory experience (variety of smells).
3. To provide a tactile experience (variety of textures/temperatures).
4. To provide an auditory experience (sound of the electrical equipment).
5. To encourage an interactive environment.
6. To encourage participation in the activity.
7. To provide an opportunity to express likes and dislikes.
8. To provide an opportunity to make choices.
9. To encourage participants to use a switch and teach them the concept of cause and effect.
10. To have fun.

Ingredients and equipment

- 7 oz (200 g) redcurrants, stalks removed*
- 7 oz (200 g) strawberries, hulled*
- 7 oz (200 g) raspberries*
- ¼ cup sugar
- 9 slices white bread (preferably 1 day old to absorb fruit juices better)
- Dash of Cointreau
- Thick cream (chilled)
- Electric frying pan

- Electric knife
- Power box
- Switches
- Chopping board
- Bowl/deep dish
- Plastic wrap (cling film)
- Serving plate
- Bowls
- Spoons
- Knife

* approx. 1 punnet of each or equal quantities

Method

1. Position group members so that they have the opportunity to greet one another, either by looking at or reaching out to each other.
2. Pass fruit around to feel and smell.
3. Use the chopping board and electric knife with power box and switch to cut strawberries, and pass around to taste. Place participants' hands on the appliance or table to feel the vibrations.
4. Pass redcurrants around to taste, unless any participants have eating difficulties.
5. Put sugar into 2 bowls and pass around – one to feel and the other to taste.
6. Place strawberries and redcurrants in the electric frying pan and sprinkle with sugar.
7. Stir gently over low heat for about 5 minutes until the sugar dissolves in the fruit juices.
8. Pass raspberries around to taste and smell.
9. Pass Cointreau around to smell and taste (unless any participants are on medication).
10. Add raspberries and Cointreau to the mixture and cook for a further 3 minutes, stirring occasionally, until the fruit has softened. Remove from heat and allow to cool.

11. While the fruit is cooking, pass bread around to taste (unless any participants have eating difficulties).

12. Use the chopping board and electric knife to cut the crusts off the bread and cut the bread into slices.

13. Line the bowl/deep dish with slices of bread on the diagonal, overlapping slightly (the sides of the bowl should be covered by bread).

14. Pour the fruit mixture into the bowl. Top with bread slices, trimmed to fit.

15. Pass the cold cream pot around to feel and taste.

16. Cover the bowl with plastic wrap, top with a saucer or plate to fit and place a weight (such as a heavy can) on top and refrigerate for at least 24 hours. (It is a good idea to put a plate under the bowl as juices may overflow – it depends on quantity.)

17. To serve, run a knife carefully between the bread and bowl, invert onto the serving plate and cut into wedges. Serve with plenty of thick cream.

18. At the end of the activity, position group members so that they have the opportunity to say goodbye to one another, either by looking at or reaching out to each other.

SWEET CHILLI SAUCE

Aims

1. To provide a gustatory experience (variety of tastes).
2. To provide an olfactory experience (variety of smells).
3. To provide a tactile experience (variety of textures).
4. To provide an auditory experience (sound of the electrical equipment).
5. To provide a visual experience (labels under UV lamp, and ribbons).
6. To encourage an interactive environment.
7. To encourage participation in the activity.
8. To provide an opportunity to express likes and dislikes.
9. To provide an opportunity to make choices.
10. To encourage participants to use a switch and teach them the concept of cause and effect.
11. To have fun.

Ingredients and equipment

These quantities make ¾ cup of sauce.

- 14 small red chillies, stems removed
- 6 cloves garlic
- 1 cup white vinegar
- ½ cup sugar
- 1 tsp salt
- Electric food processor
- Electric frying pan
- Electric knife

- Small lightweight jug
- Chopping board
- Bowls
- Bottles/jars
- Coloured, silver/gold and glittery ribbon
- White labels
- UV lamp

Method

1. Position group members so that they have the opportunity to greet one another, either by looking at or reaching out to each other.
2. Using the chopping board and electric knife or the electric food processor, roughly chop 12 chillies and 4 cloves of garlic.
3. Put the chopped chillies and garlic into a small jug and co-actively assist participants to pour them into the electric frying pan.
4. Co-actively pour in the vinegar and sugar, and add salt.
5. Bring to the boil, lower the heat and simmer until a syrupy consistency is achieved (10–15 minutes).
6. While the mixture is simmering, pass around the remaining chillies and garlic to feel and smell. Offer a very small piece of each to taste if participants can tolerate spicy tastes. Note their reactions.
7. Pour extra sugar and salt into bowls and pass around to feel and taste.
8. Pass around extra vinegar to feel, smell and taste.
9. Place the mixture in the electric food processor. Using the power box and switch, blend until the chillies are finely chopped. Place participants' hands on the appliance or table to feel the vibrations.
10. Offer participants a taste of the chilli sauce.
11. Look at the white labels under the UV lamp.
12. Pass ribbon around to feel and look at.

Sweet chilli sauce CONTINUED

13. Co-actively assist participants to pour sauce into bottles/jars and decorate. The sauce will keep for about a month if stored in a sterilised jar.

14. At the end of the activity, position group members so that they have the opportunity to say goodbye to one another, either by looking at or reaching out to each other.

Activities
PERSONAL AND HOUSEHOLD CARE

BATH SALTS

Aims

1. To provide an olfactory experience (variety of smells).
2. To provide a tactile experience (variety of textures).
3. To encourage an interactive environment.
4. To encourage participation in the activity.
5. To provide an opportunity to make choices of colours and perfumes.
6. To provide a visual experience (variety of colours together, pretty packaging).
7. To encourage co-active participation (e.g. hand skills – stirring).
8. To enjoy group work.
9. To have fun.

Materials and equipment

- Electric soda crystals
- Food colourings
- Essential oils (e.g. lavender, orange) (use 20 drops essential oil to 9 oz/250 g crystals)
- Small jars, with lids
- Wooden spoons/metal spoons
- Large metal bowl
- Cotton wool balls
- Labels
- Pressed flowers
- Ribbon
- Bowls

Method

1. Position group members so that they have the opportunity to greet one another, either by looking at or reaching out to each other.
2. Pour soda crystals into a bowl and pass around to feel.
3. Offer a choice of colours – a favourite colour or perhaps matching participants' clothing. Place several drops of food colouring on the crystals and help participants to stir them in the metal bowl.
4. Put a drop of essential oil onto a cotton wool ball and pass around to smell. Repeat with different essential oils. Note if individuals indicate a preference.
5. Add the essential oil participants appear to choose to the crystals.
6. Assist them to stir the crystals in the metal bowl. Draw their attention to the sound of the crystals and the spoon in the bowl. Comment on the change of colour and the smells.
7. Assist participants to place the crystals into the jars.
8. Pass ribbon around for them to look at and feel.
9. Place a label made with pressed flowers on each jar and tie a piece of ribbon around each.
10. At the end of the activity, position group members so that they have the opportunity to say goodbye to one another, either by looking at or reaching out to each other.

BEAUTY CARE/BODY AWARENESS

Aims

1. To provide an olfactory experience (variety of smells).
2. To provide a tactile experience (variety of textures/vibrations/temperatures).
3. To encourage participants to tolerate touch.
4. To provide a visual experience (bubbles/mirror).
5. To encourage an interactive environment.
6. To encourage participation in the activity.
7. To increase body awareness.
8. To have fun.

Materials and equipment

- Loofah
- Rubber scrub mitt
- Hairdryer
- Footspa
- Foot warmer
- Participants' own brushes/combs
- Shaving foam
- Mirror
- Massager

- Aloe vera gel
- Moisturiser
- Apricot scrub
- Japanese grains (exfoliating facial cleaner)
- Perfume/aftershave
- Talc
- Bubble bath
- Bowls of warm and cold water

Method

1. Position group members so that they have the opportunity to greet one another, either by looking at or reaching out to each other.
2. Assist them to explore the different textures, massaging the lotions, gels, shaving foam and so on into their hands, and rubbing the loofah (gently) and rubber scrub mitt against their skin. If any participants are tactile defensive and cannot tolerate the touch on their hands, start by massaging their shoulders and move down the arm using firm pressure.
3. Draw participants' attention to their body parts while working with them, giving them the opportunity to explore the different parts of their body.
4. Fill the footspa with water and take turns to place participants' feet in the water. Turn on to the massage and then bubbles settings. If participants enjoy this, leave on for a minute then turn off and encourage them to indicate to you that they want some more (e.g. by looking at you, vocalising or reaching for your hand to turn the footspa back on).
5. Assist individuals to feel the warm and cold water, and note their preferences. Look at their responses with plain water and also with bubble bath.
6. Assist participants to brush their hair, or brush it for them. Note whether they try to pull away or enjoy it.
7. Blow air from a hairdryer onto participants' hands or hair. Note their reactions.
8. Assist individuals to put their hands and feet in the foot warmer.
9. Look at participants' responses to the massager – do they prefer it on their hands/back?
10. Throughout the activity, observe whether the different stimuli stop/reduce self-engagement behaviours such as hand sucking.
11. At the end of the activity, position group members so that they have the opportunity to say goodbye to one another, either by looking at or reaching out to each other.

HAND LOTION

Aims

1. To provide a gustatory experience (variety of tastes).
2. To provide an olfactory experience (variety of smells).
3. To provide a tactile experience (variety of textures).
4. To provide an auditory experience (sound of the electrical equipment).
5. To encourage an interactive environment.
6. To encourage participation in the activity.
7. To provide an opportunity to express likes and dislikes.
8. To provide an opportunity to make choices.
9. To encourage participants to use a switch and teach them the concept of cause and effect.
10. To have fun.

Materials and equipment

- Glycerine
- Honey
- Lemons (for juice)
- Olive oil
- Electric knife
- Electric juicer
- Electric mixer
- Power box
- Switches
- Chopping board
- Spoons/measuring cups
- Glass bottles
- Labels

Method

1. Position group members so that they have the opportunity to greet one another, either by looking at or reaching out to each other.
2. Show everyone the ingredients and tell them what we are going to be making.
3. Pass a small amount of glycerine around to each participant for them to smell and taste (they should taste only a small amount as glycerine is a laxative). Rub a small amount into each participant's hand.
4. Pass honey around to smell, taste and also touch.
5. Score lemons and pass around for everyone to smell. Using the power box and switch, juice lemons in the electric juicer then pass around the lemon juice to taste.
6. Pass around olive oil to smell and taste, and rub a small amount on each participant's hand.
7. Place equal amounts of all the above ingredients into the bowl of the electric mixer. Use power box and switch to mix together until blended. Place participants' hands on the appliance or table to feel the vibrations.
8. If time permits, massage participants' hands with hand lotion.
9. Pour the remaining lotion into individual bottles for each person to take home. Label the bottles.
10. Position group members so that they have the opportunity to say goodbye to one another, either by looking at or reaching out to each other.

HAVING A BATH OR SHOWER

Aims

1. To provide an olfactory experience (variety of smells).
2. To provide a tactile experience (variety of textures/vibrations/temperatures).
3. To encourage participants to tolerate touch.
4. To provide a visual experience (bubbles).
5. To encourage an interactive environment.
6. To encourage participation in the activity.
7. To increase body awareness.
8. To have fun.

Materials and equipment

- Loofah
- Flannel
- Spa mat
- Shampoo
- Conditioner
- Soap
- Bath products (e.g. bath oil, bubble bath, bath salts)
- Large jug
- Flexi hose (for the bath)
- Moisturiser
- Deodorant
- Hair spray
- Hair gel
- Shaving foam
- Perfume/aftershave
- Towels (out of the linen closet and out of a drier)
- Hairdryer

Method

1. This is an individual activity, but still introduce it with an object symbol to let everyone know they are having a bath or shower.
2. Assist the participants to explore the different textures and smells used when having a bath or shower.
3. Experiment to see whether they prefer a bath or shower.
4. When washing hair, experiment to see whether the individual prefers to have their hair washed in the shower, or in the bath, using a jug with water to wash their hair. Some people prefer the heavy pressure of water pouring out of a jug than the 'needle spray' from a shower.
5. Draw the individual's attention to body parts while washing and drying.
6. Put the spa mat in the bath to see whether the individual enjoys the feel of the massage and looking at the bubbles.
7. When drying, use towels out of the linen closet and warm towels straight from the drier. Which do people prefer?
8. Try different techniques when drying. Do individuals prefer a firm rub or to have their bodies patted dry?
9. Assist each participant to explore the different products used after a shower.
10. Experiment to see whether individuals prefer to have their hair dried with a hairdryer (and which setting – hot or cold) or to have their hair towel-dried.
11. When you have finished the activity, and you are leaving the participant, let them know that the activity and interaction have finished.

HOMEMADE FACE PACK

Aims

1. To provide a gustatory experience (variety of tastes).
2. To provide an olfactory experience (variety of smells).
3. To provide a tactile experience (variety of textures/vibrations).
4. To provide an auditory experience (sounds of the electrical equipment).
5. To encourage an interactive environment.
6. To encourage participation in an activity.
7. To provide an opportunity to express likes and dislikes.
8. To provide the opportunity to make choices.
9. To encourage participants to use a switch and teach them the concept of cause and effect.
10. To have fun.

Materials and equipment

- Peppermint essence
- 1 egg
- 1 cucumber
- 1 lemon
- Natural thickener (e.g. cornflour)
- Bowls
- Electric blender
- Paper towels
- Power box
- Switches
- Electric egg whisk
- Electric knife
- Chopping board
- Electric juicer
- Bowls of warm and cold water
- Towels

Method

1. Position group members so that they have the opportunity to greet one another, either by looking at or reaching out to each other.
2. Assist individuals to touch and smell the different ingredients.
3. Assist one participant to break an egg (if possible); otherwise support individuals to do this and separate out the yolk and egg white.
4. Connect the electric egg whisk to power box and switch and encourage participants to operate it to whisk up the egg white. Place participants' hands on the appliance or table to feel the vibrations.
5. Use the chopping board and electric knife with the power box and switch to chop the cucumber into cubes.
6. Assist participants to place the cucumber into the blender. Using the power box and switch, encourage them to operate the blender to break up the cucumber. Offer individuals a taste of the cucumber and note their reactions.
7. Wrap cucumber in paper towel and assist group members to press down on the paper to remove any excess moisture from the cucumber.
8. Use the chopping board and electric knife to cut the lemon in half.
9. Assist participants to place half the lemon on the electric juicer and press down to feel the vibrations from the juicer.
10. Assist them to smell and taste the lemon juice. When trying to assess whether or not individuals like/dislike something, watch their reactions and offer some more to see whether they refuse.

11. Assist participants to pour the cucumber into a bowl and add the lemon juice and peppermint essence. Fold in the egg white and add the thickener to form a paste.

12. Apply a little mixture to participants' hands and check there are no adverse reactions to the ingredients. If individuals can tolerate the face pack, apply it to their faces. Massage in the mixture.

13. Encourage them to look at their reflections in the mirror with the face pack on.

14. Remove the face pack with warm/cold water – whatever each person seems to prefer.

15. At the end of the activity, position group members so that they have the opportunity to say goodbye to one another, either by looking at or reaching out to each other.

MASSAGE AND AROMATHERAPY

Before doing this activity, talk with an aromatherapist about the safe use of essential oils. Liaise with an occupational therapist or physiotherapist, masseur or aromatherapist to find out about massage techniques and contraindications.

Aims

1. To provide an opportunity to smell different oils and make choices as to which oil to use in a massage.
2. To provide a relaxing or stimulating environment as required by individuals, using the different essential oils.
3. To provide a tactile experience through massage with oils.
4. To provide a tactile experience through massage with the footspa.
5. To increase tolerance to touch for those who are tactile defensive.
6. To provide an opportunity for participants to indicate that they want more massage (e.g. through eye contact, reaching for your hand, pointing at the massage bottle/dial on the foot spa).
7. To provide an opportunity for participants to get out of their wheelchairs.

Materials and equipment

- Essential oils, e.g. lavender (relaxing), orange (calming and increases communication), lemon (stimulating), eucalyptus (good for respiratory problems)
- Carrier oil
- Measuring container
- Oil burner
- Saucers/bowls
- Cotton wool balls
- Mats
- Foot spa
- Towels
- Cassette or CD player
- Relaxing music tape or CD
- Candles/fibre-optic spray

Method

1. Light the oil burner before the activity so that the oils can diffuse through the room. Add water and 6 drops of lavender or orange to the oil burner.
2. Draw the curtains, light candles and/or turn on the fibre-optic spray to create an environment with subdued lighting. Turn on the cassette or CD player.
3. Place mats on the floor and assist 2 people out of their wheelchairs (vary the numbers according to number of support workers present).
4. Put drops of the different oils on cotton wool balls for participants to smell. Offer each person only 2 or 3 choices. Note their reactions and see whether or not you can determine which oils individuals like and dislike.
5. Using one oil that seems to be a preferred choice, mix the essential oil with carrier oil (5 drops essential oil to 10 ml carrier oil).
6. Add another preferred essential oil to the footspa.
7. Offer participants the choice of foot spa or massage with oils.
8. Warm the oil up in your hands before applying to the skin: while it is still in its bottle – *do not apply essential oils directly onto the skin.*

9. Massage participants' arms and hands, legs and feet, heads and backs. Note which part of the body people prefer to have massaged.

10. At the end of the activity, warn participants that the lights are going back on. Position group members so that they have the opportunity to say goodbye to one another, either by looking at or reaching out to each other.

You may find it useful to refer to Sanderson and Harrison with Price (1996). Their book, *Aromatherapy and Massage for People with Learning Difficulties*, sets out an interactive massage sequence and looks at multisensory massage.

PEPPERMINT FACE MASK

Aims

1. To provide a gustatory experience (variety of tastes).
2. To provide an olfactory experience (variety of smells).
3. To provide a tactile experience (variety of textures/vibrations).
4. To provide an auditory experience (sounds of the electrical equipment).
5. To encourage an interactive environment.
6. To encourage participation in an activity.
7. To provide an opportunity to express likes and dislikes.
8. To provide an opportunity to make choices.
9. To encourage participants to use a switch and teach them the concept of cause and effect.
10. To have fun.

Materials and equipment

- 2 eggs (1 for recipe)
- 1 cucumber (½ peeled cucumber for recipe)
- 1 lemon (1 tsp lemon juice for recipe)
- 1 handful fresh peppermint leaves
- Enough skimmed milk powder to bind mixture
- Tray
- Bowls

- Electric knife
- Electric food processor/blender
- Electric juicer
- Power box
- Switches
- Bowls of warm water
- Flannels
- Towels
- Mirror

Method

1. Position group members so that they have the opportunity to greet one another, either by looking at or reaching out to each other.
2. Break one of the eggs on a tray and pass around to feel and look at.
3. Use the electric knife with power box and switch to peel the skin off the cucumber.
4. Pass cucumber around to smell and feel.
5. Cut the lemon with the electric knife then juice in the electric juicer. Encourage participants to place their hands on the juicer or table to feel the vibrations.
6. Pass lemon juice around to smell and taste.
7. Pass peppermint leaves around to smell and feel.
8. Put skimmed milk powder in bowls and pass around to smell and feel.
9. Mix all ingredients together in the electric food processor/blender until a thick cream is formed.
10. Try a small dab of cream on the inside of participants' elbows to check whether they react to the ingredients.
11. If participants are not sensitive to the cream, first massage onto hands and then face if individuals permit. Leave on for a few minutes.
12. Participants should be encouraged to look at themselves in the mirror with the face mask on.
13. Wash off with warm water then pat dry.
14. At the end of the activity, position group members so that they have the opportunity to say goodbye to one another, either by looking at or reaching out to each other.

POTPOURRI

Aims

1. To provide an olfactory experience (variety of smells).
2. To provide a tactile experience (variety of textures).
3. To encourage an interactive environment.
4. To encourage participation in the activity.
5. To provide an opportunity to express likes and dislikes.
6. To provide an opportunity to make choices.
7. To have fun.

Materials and equipment

- 1 packet wood shavings
- 1 packet potpourri mix
- Essential oils (e.g. lavender, lemon, orange, sandalwood)
- Envelopes
- Rubber stamps with motifs (and adapted handles)
- Inks
- Gold/silver pens
- Cotton wool balls/tissues
- Small jug
- Bowls
- Small baskets/bowls

Method

1. Position group members so that they can greet one another, either by looking at or reaching out to each other.
2. Assist participants to pass around the packets of wood shavings and potpourri mix to feel.
3. Open the packets and pour into bowls. Pass around the wood shavings and dried flowers to feel.
4. Offer participants the choice of wood shavings or dried flowers (individuals may make a choice by looking at the one they want).
5. Put drops of the essential oils on the cotton wool balls or tissues and pass around to smell. Note individuals' reactions and try to interpret which oil they prefer/dislike. Mix the preferred oil with the chosen wood shavings/dried flowers.
6. Offer participants the choice of different motifs and help each person to stamp their chosen picture onto an envelope.
7. Offer participants the choice of silver or gold pen, and write individuals' names on the envelopes, along with the name of their chosen essential oil.
8. Put the wood shavings/dried flowers in a small jug and co-actively assist participants to pour the contents into the envelopes.
9. Seal the envelopes and use in wardrobes or drawers. Alternatively, find small baskets/ decorative bowls and keep the potpourri on the table.
10. At the end of the activity, position group members so that they can say goodbye to one another, either by looking at or reaching out to each other.

REFRESHING PEPPERMINT FOOT CREAM

Aims

1. To provide a gustatory experience (variety of tastes).
2. To provide an olfactory experience (variety of smells).
3. To provide a tactile experience (variety of textures).
4. To provide an auditory experience (sound of the electrical equipment).
5. To provide a visual experience.
6. To encourage an interactive environment.
7. To encourage participation in the activity.
8. To provide an opportunity to express likes and dislikes.
9. To provide an opportunity to make choices.
10. To encourage participants to use a switch and teach them the concept of cause and effect.
11. To have fun.

Materials and equipment

The following quantities make 5–8 small tubs of cream.

- 500 ml unfragranced moisturising cream
- 1 lemon (for 1 tbsp juice)
- 2 tsp vodka
- 1 tbsp peppermint oil
- Small cosmetic tubs
- Fluorescent paper (for labels)
- Ultraviolet lamp
- Cups
- Cotton wool balls

- Glue or tape
- Teaspoons
- Bowls
- Electric knife
- Electric blender
- Power box
- Switches
- Chopping board
- Electric juicer

Method

1. Position group members so that they have an opportunity to greet one another, either by looking at or reaching out to each other.
2. Score the lemon using the electric knife with power box and switch to release the aroma, and pass around to feel and smell. Place participants' hands on the appliance or table to feel the vibrations.
3. Remove the rind and cut the lemon into segments using the chopping board and electric knife.
4. Use switch-operated electric juicer to juice the lemon.
5. Place 1 tablespoon of lemon juice into the electric blender. Pass the remaining juice around to taste.
6. Pour the vodka into a cup. Pass around to smell and taste from teaspoons. Do not offer vodka to anyone who is on medication.
7. Place 2 teaspoons of vodka into the blender.
8. Put some of the peppermint oil onto a cotton wool ball and pass around to smell. Add 1 tablespoon of the oil to the blender.
9. Pass some of the moisturising cream around to feel and massage into participants' hands. Place the remainder into the blender with other ingredients.
10. Use the blender with the power box and switch to blend all ingredients together well.

11. Put some of the completed cream into a bowl. Pass around to feel and smell. Massage into participants' hands and feet.

12. Encourage group members to choose the colour of fluorescent paper that they would like for their label. Shine a UV light onto the paper to enhance its brightness.

13. Write on the labels and secure on cosmetic tubs with glue or tape.

14. Spoon the completed foot cream into individual tubs.

15. At the end of the activity, position group members so that they have the opportunity to say goodbye to one another, either by looking at or reaching out to each other.

RICH YOGHURT AND FRUIT EXFOLIATING MASK

Aims

1. To provide a gustatory experience (variety of tastes).
2. To provide an olfactory experience (variety of smells).
3. To provide a tactile experience (variety of textures/vibrations).
4. To provide an auditory experience (sounds from the electrical equipment).
5. To encourage an interactive environment.
6. To encourage participation in an activity.
7. To provide an opportunity to express likes and dislikes.
8. To provide an opportunity to make choices.
9. To encourage participants to use a switch and teach them the concept of cause and effect.
10. To have fun.

Materials and equipment

- 2 large ripe peaches (1 for recipe) – as an alternative use kiwi fruit or papaya
- 1 tsp honey
- 1 tsp cold yoghurt
- 2 tsp oatmeal
- Electric knife
- Electric food processor/blender
- Chopping board
- Power box
- Switches
- Bowls of warm water
- Flannels
- Towels
- Bowls
- Teaspoons
- Mirror

Method

1. Position group members so that they have the opportunity to greet one another, either by looking at or reaching out to each other.
2. Pass around peach to smell and feel.
3. Peel the peaches on a chopping board, using the electric knife, power box and switches. Cut into pieces and pass around to taste and smell. If using kiwi fruit or papaya instead of peach, do the same with these.
4. Pass around honey to smell and taste.
5. Pass around yoghurt to smell, taste and feel.
6. Put oatmeal into a bowl and pass around to feel.
7. Blend the chosen fruit, honey and yoghurt in the electric blender, then add the oatmeal to make a paste. Encourage participants to put their hands on the blender or table to feel the vibrations.
8. Try a small dab of cream on the inside of participants' elbows to check whether they react to the ingredients.
9. If individuals are not sensitive to the cream, first massage onto their hands and then face if individuals permit. Leave on for a few minutes.
10. Participants should be encouraged to look at themselves in the mirror with the face mask on.
11. Wash off with warm water then pat dry.
12. At the end of the activity, position group members so that they have the opportunity to say goodbye to one another, either by looking at or reaching out to each other.

RUM AND EGG SHAMPOO ADDITIVE

This can be used to restore body to fine or limp hair.

Aims

1. To provide a tactile experience (variety of textures).
2. To provide an olfactory experience (variety of smells).
3. To provide a gustatory experience (variety of tastes).
4. To provide an auditory experience (sound of the electrical equipment).
5. To encourage an interactive environment.
6. To encourage participation in the activity.
7. To provide an opportunity to express likes and dislikes.
8. To provide an opportunity to make choices.
9. To encourage participants to use a switch and teach them the concept of cause and effect.
10. To have fun.

Materials and equipment

- Shampoo
- White rum
- 2 eggs (1 for recipe)
- Peppermint essence
- Power box
- Switches
- Electric blender
- Bowls
- Chopping board/tray
- Teaspoons
- Small jug
- Small bottles
- Ribbon (different types/colours)

Method

1. Position group members so that they can greet one another, either by looking at or reaching out to each other.
2. Assist participants to pour shampoo into the bowl co-actively.
3. Pass the bowl around to feel and smell the shampoo.
4. Pass around white rum to smell and taste. Do not offer to any individuals who are on medication.
5. Pass around 1 egg to feel. Break the egg on board/tray and pass around to feel – watch how it runs on the tray.
6. Pass around peppermint essence to smell and taste.
7. Put all ingredients in the electric blender and use the power box and switch to mix all ingredients (ratio: 1 cup shampoo, 1 tablespoon rum, 1 egg, 1 teaspoon peppermint). Place participants' hands on the appliance or table to feel the vibrations.
8. Using the small jug, assist participants to pour shampoo mixture into small bottles.
9. Pass ribbon around to feel. Decorate bottles with the ribbon that individuals have chosen.
10. Use shampoo as usual. Store and refrigerate; discard after 5 days.
11. At the end of the activity, position group members so that they have the opportunity to say goodbye to one another, either by looking at or reaching out to each other.

SCENTED DRAWER LINERS

Aims

1. To provide an olfactory experience (variety of smells).
2. To provide a tactile experience (different textures/vibrations).
3. To provide an auditory experience (sound of the electrical equipment).
4. To provide a visual experience (looking at the drawer liners).
5. To encourage an interactive environment.
6. To encourage participation in the activity.
7. To provide an opportunity to express likes and dislikes.
8. To provide an opportunity to make choices.
9. To encourage participants to use a switch and teach them the concept of cause and effect.
10. To have fun.

Materials and equipment

- 2 pieces of paper the same size as the drawer (e.g. brown paper, butcher's paper or recycled gift wrap)
- 1 tbsp nutmeg (plus extra to feel)
- 1 tbsp whole cloves (plus extra to feel)
- 1 tbsp cinnamon sticks (plus extra to feel)
- 1 tbsp scented oil
- 2 tbsp PVA glue

- Electric nut grinder/ food processor
- Power box
- Switches
- Paint brush
- Bowls
- Scissors
- Tablespoon

Method

1. Position group members so that they have the opportunity to greet one another, either by looking at or reaching out to each other.
2. Grind the nutmeg, cloves and cinnamon sticks in the electric grinder/food processor, operated using the power box and switch. Place participants' hands on the appliance or table to feel the vibrations.
3. Encourage participants to listen to the sounds of the spices being ground.
4. Pass extra amounts of the spices around to smell and feel.
5. Pass the scented oil around to smell.
6. Sprinkle the scented oil in with the spices and add the glue – pass around to smell.
7. Use the food processor to mix the ingredients thoroughly.
8. Use a paint brush to coat the back of one piece of paper with the mixture.
9. Press the second piece of paper onto this and leave to dry.
10. At the end of the activity, position group members so that they have the opportunity to say goodbye to one another, either by looking at or reaching out to each other.

SHOE CLEANING

Aims

1. To provide an olfactory experience (variety of smells).
2. To provide a tactile experience (variety of textures).
3. To provide an auditory experience (sound of brushes).
4. To encourage an interactive environment.
5. To encourage participation in the activity.
6. To provide an opportunity to express likes and dislikes.
7. To provide an opportunity to make choices.
8. To provide an opportunity to be involved in an everyday activity.
9. To have fun.

Materials and equipment

- Shoe polish
- Dubbin (waterproof polish)
- Brushes (hard and soft)
- Cloths
- Shoes

Method

1. Position group members so that they have the opportunity to greet one another, either by looking at or reaching out to each other.
2. Pass cloths and brushes around to feel.
3. Put shoe polish on a cloth and rub onto a shoe.
4. Use the hard brush to brush the shoes. Allow participants to feel the brush again and experiment with the different noises it makes being brushed on different surfaces and against the soft brush.
5. Take off the shoe polish using the soft brush and experiment again, as with the hard brush.
6. Pass a soft cloth around to feel then polish the shoe with the soft cloth.
7. Put the dubbin or other waterproof grease on the cloth. Rub into the shoe.
8. Experiment with other shoe-cleaning products and materials.
9. At the end of the activity, position group members so that they have the opportunity to say goodbye to one another, either by looking at or reaching out to each other.

SOAP BALLS

Aims

1. To provide an olfactory experience (variety of smells).
2. To provide a tactile experience (variety of textures).
3. To provide an auditory experience (sound of the electrical equipment).
4. To encourage an interactive environment.
5. To encourage participation in the activity.
6. To provide an opportunity to express likes and dislikes.
7. To provide an opportunity to make choices.
8. To encourage participants to use a switch and teach them the concept of cause and effect.
9. To have fun.

Materials and equipment

- Soap powder (from craft shops) or soap flakes (for wool washing); use hot water to dissolve
- Essential oils (e.g. lavender, orange, pine)
- Cotton wool balls
- Water
- Coloured food dyes
- Textures (e.g. barley bran, wheatgerm)
- Spice powder
- Electic water pourer
- Electric blender
- Power box
- Switches
- Freezer bags/jars
- Metal bowls
- Metal spoon
- Tablespoon
- Cup

Method

1. Position group members so that they have the opportunity to greet one another, either by looking at or reaching out to each other.
2. Put soap powder/flakes in bowls and pass around to feel.
3. Put essential oils onto cotton wool balls and pass around to smell. Note individuals' reactions to determine which essential oil they prefer.
4. Divide soap powder into individual bowls and add the chosen essential oils.
5. Mix together using a metal spoon and listen to the sound of metal on metal.
6. Put barley bran/wheatgerm in bowls and pass around to feel.
7. Pass around spice powder to smell.
8. Add the barley bran/wheatgerm and spice powder to the soap powder to give texture to the soap.
9. Place the mixture in the electric blender, and mix using the power box and switch (use 2 or 3 cups soap powder to 1 tablespoon water). Place participants' hands on the appliance or table to feel the vibrations. Add colour to soap powder if desired. Add water to the mixture, using the electric water pourer. Adjust the water content so that a firm texture is achieved and the soap can be shaped into balls.
10. Set the soap aside to dry for 24–48 hours.
11. Put soap balls in resealable freezer bags or small jars.
12. At the end of the activity, position group members so that they have the opportunity to say goodbye to one another, either by looking at or reaching out to each other.

STRAWBERRY ALMOND FACIAL SCRUB

Aims

1. To provide a tactile experience (variety of textures/vibrations/temperatures).
2. To provide an olfactory experience (variety of smells).
3. To provide a gustatory experience (variety of tastes).
4. To provide an auditory experience (sounds of the electrical equipment).
5. To encourage an interactive environment.
6. To encourage participation in the activity.
7. To provide an opportunity to express likes and dislikes.
8. To provide an opportunity to make choices.
9. To encourage participants to use a switch and teach them the concept of cause and effect.
10. To have fun.

Materials and equipment

- ½ peeled, chopped cucumber (refresher)
- Punnet strawberries (cleanser, conditioner)
- 1 tbsp baking soda (cleanser)
- 3 eggs (toner, binder)
- Natural yoghurt (conditioner)
- Almonds (exfoliator)
- Bowls cold and warm water
- Power box

- Switches
- Electric knife
- Electric blender
- Electric grinder
- Chopping board
- Spoons
- Bowls
- Tray
- Mirror

Method

1. Position group members so that they have the opportunity to greet one another, either by looking at or reaching out to each other.
2. Using the chopping board and power box with switch, cut the cucumber with the electric knife and pass around to feel, smell and taste. Place participants' hands on the appliance or table to feel the vibrations.
3. Pass strawberries around to feel, taste and smell (keep 5 aside for the facial scrub).
4. Put baking soda in a bowl and pass around to feel.
5. Put yoghurt in 2 bowls and pass 1 around to feel and the other to smell and taste (keep 2 heaped tablespoons for facial scrub).
6. Pass around an egg to feel. Break the egg on the tray and pass around to feel.
7. Put almonds in a bowl and pass around to feel.
8. Place almonds in the electric grinder or electric blender and use the power box and switch to grind the almonds (⅔ cup is needed for the facial scrub). Place participants' hands on the blender or table to feel the vibrations.
9. Place the cucumber and strawberries in the electric blender and purée using the power box and switch.
10. Add the baking soda, eggs and yoghurt and blend on low power.
11. Add the ground almonds and blend for a further 2 minutes.
12. Pass around bowls of warm and cold water for participants to feel. Note their reactions.
13. Try a small dab of cream on the inside of the participants' elbows to check whether they react to the ingredients.

14. Moisten participants' faces and/or hands then apply the scrub using a gentle circular motion. Do not use on face if the skin is sensitive. Leave on for a few minutes.

15. Participants should be encouraged to look at themselves in the mirror with the facial scrub on.

16. Rinse with warm water, then cold water to close the pores.

17. At the end of the activity, position group members so that they have the opportunity to say goodbye to one another, either by looking at or reaching out to each other.

SWEET VIOLET HAND CREAM

Aims

1. To provide an olfactory experience (variety of smells).
2. To provide a tactile experience (different textures/consistencies).
3. To provide an auditory experience (sound of the electrical equipment).
4. To provide a visual experience (looking at the glitter).
5. To encourage an interactive environment.
6. To encourage participation in the activity.
7. To provide an opportunity to express likes and dislikes.
8. To provide an opportunity to make choices.
9. To encourage participants to use a switch and teach them the concept of cause and effect.
10. To have fun.

Materials and equipment

- 1 tsp beeswax
- 3 tbsp almond oil
- Heatproof bowl
- Small saucepan
- Newspaper
- ½ tsp cornflour
- 2 tbsp boiling water
- Electric whisk
- Electric food processor
- Power box
- Switches
- 6 drops violet essential oil
- Cotton wool balls
- Presentation jar
- Labels

Method

1. Position group members so that they have the opportunity to greet one another, either by looking at or reaching out to each other.
2. Melt the beeswax in the almond oil in a bowl over a saucepan of hot water.
3. When melted, remove the bowl and stand on some folded newspaper. (This can be done in the kitchen prior to the activity. Ensure that it is not melted too early otherwise the beeswax will set again.)
4. Pass some solid beeswax, almond oil and cornflour around to smell and feel.
5. Add cornflour to the melted beeswax and almond oil, stir well and then add the water gradually, beating with the whisk until the mixture becomes creamy. Alternatively, mix in an electric food processor using a power box and switch. Place participants' hands on the appliance or table to feel the vibrations.
6. Put a drop of violet essential oil on a cotton wool ball and pass around to smell.
7. Add the violet essential oil to the mixture and continue to whisk until the cream is cool.
8. Pass around some of the cream to feel and smell.
9. Pour the rest into the presentation jar and leave to set.
10. Label with a list of ingredients or make up own labels with pressed flowers.
11. At the end of the activity, position group members so that they have the opportunity to say goodbye to one another, either by looking at or reaching out to each other.

WOOL MIX

Aims

1. To provide an olfactory experience (variety of smells).
2. To provide a tactile experience (variety of textures/temperatures).
3. To provide a visual experience (UV lamp).
4. To encourage an interactive environment.
5. To encourage participation in the activity.
6. To provide an opportunity to express likes and dislikes.
7. To provide an opportunity to make choices.
8. To have fun.

Materials and equipment

- 1 cup methylated spirits
- 2 oz (50 ml) eucalyptus
- 4 cups soap flakes (for wool washing)
- Hot and cold water
- Bowls
- Cotton wool/tissues
- Small jars
- Decorations (e.g. coloured and glittery ribbon)
- White labels
- UV lamp

Method

1. Position group members so that they have the opportunity to greet one another, either by looking at or reaching out to each other.
2. Pour the soap flakes into a bowl and pass around to feel.
3. Pass around bowls of hot and cold water to enable participants to experience the different temperatures.
4. Mix the soap flakes and water and pass around to feel.
5. Put eucalyptus onto cotton wool/tissues and pass around to smell. Note participants' reactions. Do not use eucalyptus with individuals who may swallow it.
6. Mix the methylated spirits, soap flakes and eucalyptus. Do not use methylated spirits with individuals who may swallow it.
7. Pass ribbon around to look at and feel.
8. Look at the white labels under the UV lamp.
9. Put the wool mix into small jars and decorate with the ribbon and labels.
10. Add a handful of wool mix to a bucket of water. Soak woollens in the mix then wring out and dry. No need to rinse.
11. At the end of the activity, position group members so that they have the opportunity to say goodbye to one another, either by looking at or reaching out to each other.

Activities
ART AND CRAFT

BIRD CAKE

Aims

1. To provide a gustatory experience (variety of tastes).
2. To provide an olfactory experience (variety of smells).
3. To provide a tactile experience (variety of textures).
4. To provide an auditory experience (sounds of the electrical equipment/seeds in bowl).
5. To provide an interactive environment.
6. To encourage participation in the activity.
7. To provide an opportunity to express likes and dislikes.
8. To provide an opportunity to make choices.
9. To encourage participants to use a switch and teach them the concept of cause and effect.
10. To have fun.

Materials and equipment

- Bread
- Apple
- Carrot
- Nuts
- Bacon rind
- Bird seed
- Dried fruit
- Fat
- Electric knife
- Electric frying pan
- Electric food processor
- Power box
- Switches
- Chopping board
- Small jug
- Bowls
- Cake tin/empty milk carton/plastic cup

Method

1. Position group members so that they have the opportunity to greet one another, either by looking at or reaching out to each other.
2. Pass bread around to feel and taste.
3. Pass apple around to feel.
4. Pass carrot around to feel.
5. Chop or grate the apple using the chopping board, power box and switch with electric knife or food processor. Place participants' hands on the appliance or table to feel the vibrations. Pass the apple around to smell and taste (do not offer pieces of apple to individuals with eating difficulties – offer as grated or stewed apple instead).
6. Grate the carrot using the electric food processor and pass around to smell and taste (do not offer carrot to individuals with eating difficulties).
7. Check whether any participants have nut allergies. Put nuts in bowls and pass around to feel and taste (do not offer to individuals with eating difficulties). Monitor participants feeling the nuts if they are likely to put one in their mouth but can't chew. If anyone is likely to choke on a nut, offer finely ground nuts to taste, but first check with a speech pathologist whether or not the participant can tolerate finely ground nuts.
8. Pass bacon around to feel. Using the chopping board, power box, switch and electric knife, cut off the rind and chop into pieces using the electric knife or food processor.
9. Co-actively assist participants to pour bird seed into bowls and pass around to feel (again, monitor that they do not put the seed in their mouths).

10. Co-actively pour dried fruit into bowls and pass around to feel and taste (do not offer to any individuals with eating difficulties).

11. Co-actively pour all the ingredients into the electric food processor and mix.

12. Place the fat in the electric frying pan and melt, then pour into the electric food processor and mix. Add enough fat so that all the ingredients bind together.

13. Pour the mixture into a cake tin or plastic cup and press down firmly.

14. Alternatively, roll into balls and place inside the milk carton. The carton should have large windows cut into the sides so that birds can fly in and out. As a separate project, these carton bird feeders can be decorated (e.g. with paint or different materials).

15. After the bird cake has set, cut it from the cake tin or remove it from the plastic cup and put it outside. Encourage participants to watch the birds eating the bird cake.

16. At the end of the activity, position group members so that they have the opportunity to say goodbye to one another, either by looking at or reaching out to each other.

BUBBLEBREW (BUBBLE-BLOWING LIQUID)

Aims

1. To provide a visual experience (watching/tracking bubbles).
2. To provide an olfactory experience (variety of smells).
3. To provide a tactile experience (variety of textures).
4. To provide an auditory experience (sound of the electrical equipment).
5. To encourage an interactive environment.
6. To encourage participation in the activity.
7. To provide an opportunity to express likes and dislikes.
8. To provide an opportunity to make choices.
9. To encourage participants to use a switch and teach them the concept of cause and effect.
10. To have fun.

Materials and equipment

- 2 cups dishwashing liquid (if using concentrate use ¼ cup)
- 6 cups water
- ¼ cup glycerine
- Bowls warm and cold water
- Power box
- Switches
- Electric mixer
- Bubble mix

- Bubble wands/gun (some bubble guns can be switch-adapted using a battery interrupter)
- Bowls
- Mixing bowl
- Large spoon
- Jug
- Measuring cups

Method

1. Position group members so that they have the opportunity to greet one another, either by looking at or reaching out to each other.
2. Pass around bottle of dishwashing liquid for participants to smell and feel (encourage them to pass to one another independently or co-actively).
3. Pour liquid into a measuring cup (encourage participants to pour using co-active techniques if necessary; if anyone finds it difficult to hold and pour from the bottle, pour from a jug).
4. Pass around bowls of warm and cold water for everyone to feel.
5. Pour dishwashing liquid into a mixing bowl and add water.
6. Measure out glycerine and add to the mixture.
7. Mix using a large spoon, or place in the electric mixer and blend using power box and switch. Place participants' hands on the appliance or table to feel the vibrations.
8. Pass the bowl of bubble mix around for participants to feel.
9. Leave to settle for a few hours and use at a later date.
10. Use bubble mix that has already been made up to blow bubbles with the bubble wands/gun.
11. Encourage participants to watch/track bubbles and reach out for them. Blow some bubbles so that they land on individuals' hands and faces.
12. At the end of the activity, position group members so that they have the opportunity to say goodbye to one another, either by looking at or reaching out to each other.

CHRISTMAS TREE CARDS

This activity can also be done on a larger scale, to create a Christmas tree mural. The activity requires support workers to put the mural/cards together, but everyone is involved in making the individual parts of the cards or mural.

Aims

1. To provide an olfactory experience (variety of smells).
2. To provide a tactile experience (different textures/vibrations).
3. To provide an auditory experience (sound of the electrical equipment).
4. To provide a visual experience (looking at the silver/gold spray paint, foil paper, finished tree).
5. To encourage an interactive environment.
6. To encourage participation in the activity.
7. To provide an opportunity to express likes and dislikes.
8. To provide an opportunity to make choices.
9. To encourage participants to use a switch and teach them the concept of cause and effect.
10. To have fun.

Materials and equipment

- Hessian
- Strong card/wood
- Green paint
- Juniper oil/fragrant pine (do not use with individuals who may drink the oils)
- Coconut
- Pine needles
- PVA glue
- Pasta shapes (a variety of small shapes for cards, large for the mural)
- Silver or gold spray paint
- Coloured construction paper (for the cards)
- Bark (visit the local park to collect bark)
- Rolling pin
- Scissors
- Newspaper

- Food processor
- Power box
- Switches
- Bowls
  Extra materials for mural
- Plastic bags
- Thin cardboard
- Different-coloured foil paper
- Sandpaper
- Paper
- Cinnamon sticks, nutmeg, cardamom pods
- Red material
- Needle and thread
- Cotton wool
- Corn syrup

Method

1. Position group members so that they have the opportunity to greet one another, either by looking at or reaching out to each other.
2. Pass the different materials around for the participants to feel and smell.
3. Put pasta shapes on a piece of newspaper and help participants to spray with gold or silver paint.
4. When dry, help participants to glue the pasta shapes onto the hessian in rows or any preferred arrangement.

5. While the glue is drying cut a triangle of hessian to represent a Christmas tree shape. Cut out individual trees for each card. If doing a mural, glue onto a strong piece of board or wood. Pass the hessian around for participants to feel.

6. Use the power box and switch with the electric food processor to mix green paint with glue, juniper oil, coconut and pine needles. Cut out individual trees for each card. Place participants' hands on the processor or table to feel the vibrations.

7. Use fingers or adapted paint brushes to paint the hessian with the green paint mixture.

8. Help participants to glue the hessian tree with pasta shapes onto card for a tactile effect.

9. Glue bark at the bottom of the tree to represent the trunk and pass around to feel.

10. If making the mural, add presents beneath the tree. Make by covering plastic bags with card and foil, which give a 'scrunchy' sound when touched. Pass card and foil around to feel and listen to the sound of the foil when scrunched.

11. Pass the sandpaper around to feel. (If using coarse grained sandpaper, supervise participants so they don't graze themselves.) Tie sticks of cinnamon together with an elastic band and scratch against the sandpaper to release the smell. Some participants may be able to hold a piece of nutmeg to do this, or roll cardamom pods over the sandpaper either using hands or a rolling pin. Cut the sandpaper into star shapes and stick onto the Christmas tree.

12. Make holly leaves by painting paper with corn syrup mixed with green paint. Participants can use their hands or adapted paint brushes. When dry, cut into holly leaf shapes.

13. Make red berries for the holly by cutting circles out of the red material. Some participants may be able to sew around the edges to make a drawstring bag. Put cotton wool with drops of oil inside the bags and stick them onto the holly leaves.

14. At the end of the activity, position group members so that they have the opportunity to say goodbye to one another, either by looking at or reaching out to each other.

CINNAMON CLAY ORNAMENTS

Experiment with this activity by changing the sensory components of the clay, using nutmeg, cloves and other spices. If using nutmeg, grind in a nut grinder.

Aims

1. To provide a tactile experience (different textures/consistencies).
2. To provide an olfactory experience (variety of smells).
3. To provide an auditory experience (sounds of the electrical equipment, nuts being ground).
4. To provide a visual experience (looking at the ribbon).
5. To encourage an interactive environment.
6. To encourage participation in the activity.
7. To provide an opportunity to express likes and dislikes.
8. To provide an opportunity to make choices.
9. To encourage participants to use a switch and teach them the concept of cause and effect.
10. To have fun.

Materials and equipment

- 1 cup cinnamon
- ¼ cup white glue
- Nutmeg, cloves and other spices
- ¼ to ½ cup water
- Nut grinder
- Food processor

- Power box
- Switches
- Rolling pin
- Christmas cookie cutter shapes
- Ribbon
- Pencil or drinking straw

Method

1. Preheat the oven to 100°C (200°F).
2. Position group members so that they have the opportunity to greet one another, either by looking at or reaching out to each other.
3. Pass the different materials around to smell and feel.
4. Mix the cinnamon, glue, spices and water in a bowl until a soft ball is formed, or mix in an electric food processor using a power box and switch. Place participants' hands on the appliance or table to feel the vibrations.
5. Roll out the clay using a rolling pin until it is the thickness of your finger.
6. Press shapes out of the clay with cookie cutters. These may need to be adapted with a wooden vertical or T-bar handle.
7. Make a small hole in each shape with a straw or a pencil.
8. Place the ornament shapes in the warm oven and turn them every 5 to 10 minutes until firm.
9. Offer participants different types of ribbon to feel and look at.
10. While the ornaments are cooking, clean up. Assist participants to wipe the table and feel the bubbles in the washing-up water.
11. For each ornament, place the ribbon through the hole and tie into a bow. Hang and enjoy!
12. At the end of the activity, position group members so that they have the opportunity to say goodbye to one another, either by looking at or reaching out to each other.

CINNAMON SPICE DOUGH

Aims

1. To provide a tactile experience (variety of textures/consistencies).
2. To provide an olfactory experience (variety of smells).
3. To provide an auditory experience (sounds of the electrical equipment).
4. To encourage an interactive environment.
5. To encourage participation in the activity.
6. To provide an opportunity to express likes and dislikes.
7. To provide an opportunity to make choices.
8. To encourage participants to use a switch and teach them the concept of cause and effect.
9. To have fun.

Materials and equipment

- 2 cups flour
- 1 cup salt
- 5 tsp cinnamon
- ¾ to 1 cup warm water
- Bowl or shallow dish for mixing
- Electric food processor
- Power box
- Switches
- Board
- Plastic wrap
- Christmas ribbon
- Cookie cutters

Method

1. Position group members so that they have the opportunity to greet one another, either by looking at or reaching out to each other.
2. Pass the different materials around to smell and feel.
3. Help participants to mix flour, salt and cinnamon in a bowl using hands, or in an electric food processor using a power box and switch. Place participants' hands on the appliance or table to feel the vibrations.
4. Make a well in the centre of the mixture and help participants pour water into the bowl or add water to the electric food processor.
5. Use hands to mix until the dough forms a ball or mix in the electric food processor using a power box and switch. Add more flour or water as necessary, so the dough is not crumbly or sticky.
6. Assist participants to knead for 5 minutes on a lightly floured board until smooth and satiny, or continue to mix in the electric food processor.
7. Keep some of the clay out to explore. Wrap the rest in plastic and refrigerate for 20 minutes before using like any clay.
8. While the clay is in the fridge, explore the remainder of the clay by feeling, kneading and cutting shapes out of it. Discard when finished. Clean up any equipment used.
9. After 20 minutes, take the clay out of the fridge. Assist participants to roll out some dough 1 cm thick and cut out shapes with adapted cookie cutters with large handles.
10. Roll the rest to make candy cane shapes.
11. Bake in the oven at 180°C (350°F) for 1 hour, until hard.
12. Thread ribbon through to hang or use to decorate wreaths.
13. At the end of the activity, position group members so that they have the opportunity to say goodbye to one another, either by looking at or reaching out to each other.

FLOWERS AND LEAVES COLLAGE

Aims

1. To provide a tactile experience (variety of textures).
2. To provide an olfactory experience (smelling the different flowers and herbs).
3. To provide a visual experience.
4. To provide an auditory experience.
5. To encourage individuals to participate and interact with each other (e.g. passing objects around the group).
6. To provide an opportunity to express likes and dislikes.
7. To provide an opportunity to make choices.
8. To have fun and explore.

Materials and equipment

- Cling film
- Flowers – soft (e.g. proteas), with a lot of petals
- Herbs
- Leaves – large/small, dried and fresh
- Board/thick cardboard
- Bowls/baskets
- Laminator (as an alternative to cling film)

Method

1. Position group members so that they have the opportunity to greet one another, either by looking at or reaching out to each other.
2. Pass around the bowls/baskets of flowers and leaves and encourage participants to explore by feeling and smelling the different items.
3. Fan individuals with the big leaves and watch their reaction.
4. Stroke people's hands and faces with the different flowers and leaves – some proteas are soft and good for stroking the face.
5. Assist participants to pull the petals off the flowers and drop these into a bowl.
6. Encourage each person to feel the petals in the bowl, then assist them to pass the bowl on to the next person.
7. Encourage participants to feel the cling film and listen to the noise it makes (pull finger along stretched cling film to make it squeak).
8. Place one piece of cling film on the board/cardboard and wrap the ends over to keep it in place.
9. Assist participants to pick up the petals and sprinkle them over the cling film. Alternatively, keep some flowers and leaves whole and arrange them in a pattern on the cling film.
10. When the cling film is covered with petals, place another piece of cling film on top and seal up the edges.
11. Remove from the board/cardboard and stick onto the window.
12. Assist participants to move over to the window and look at the light shining through the collage.
13. If there is access to a laminator, use this instead of the cling film for a more permanent display. If using the laminator, use small, flat flowers; it may be necessary to dry them first. If they are too thick, it will be difficult to pass them through the laminator.
14. At the end of the activity, position group members so that they have the opportunity to say goodbye to one another, either by looking at or reaching out to each other.

FLUORESCENT ACTION PAINTING

Aims

1. To provide a tactile experience (variety of textures/temperatures).
2. To provide an olfactory experience (variety of smells).
3. To provide a visual experience (different colours, tin foil).
4. To provide an interactive environment.
5. To encourage participation in an activity.
6. To provide an opportunity to express likes and dislikes.
7. To provide an opportunity to make choices.
8. To encourage participants to use a switch and teach them the concept of cause and effect.
9. To have fun.

Materials and equipment

- White nylon tulle or coarse plain net or fine, sheer white nylon
- Fluorescent acrylic paints (water soluble, non toxic) – 4 different colours
- Masking tape
- Disposable gloves
- White dishes to mix paints
- Non-slip mats
- Coarse paint brushes, rollers, long-handled brushes
- Plastic bags
- Cleaning materials
- Water
- UV lamp/room

NB: White nylon will fluoresce under dark light. Tulle and coarse net will form a soft sculpture as it can be bundled loosely on the floor. Finer net can be hung and draped from the wall and lines. Both materials look solid and sculptural under dark light and can become an additional resource for the darkroom once they have been displayed.

Method

1. Position group members so that they have the opportunity to greet each other, either by looking at or reaching out to each other.
2. Pass materials and tape around for them to feel and look at under UV light.
3. Tape materials to the floor.
4. Look at paints under UV light and offer participants a choice of colour.
5. Put each paint in a white dish and mix in water to dilute.
6. Apply paint to the net.
7. The paint can be applied in a number of ways, depending on ability, choices and preferences about getting messy:
   (a) put paint onto a wheelchair tyre, then wheel forward onto the net
   (b) paint using bare feet, or holding brushes or rollers with feet
   (c) paint another person's foot or hand, then indicate where they should put their footprint
   (d) have your foot or hand painted, then print with it
   (e) apply paint with a plastic bag tied over the foot (with or without shoes)
   (f) apply paint with a plastic bag tied over a broom or other long-handled tool
   (g) bend over and reach the ground with a paint brush or roller.

8. Offer painters the chance to try 2 or more ways of applying paint, and be willing to let them take control (e.g. let someone paint your foot or hand).

9. Once the painting is complete, the painters can put the net to dry and clean the floor, themselves and the wheelchairs. Acrylic paint cleans up easily if it is done quickly, before it dries completely.

10. Next, take the net through to the darkroom and display under dark light. Encourage the painters to try different ways to bundle or hang the material (e.g. drape it over a chair, stool or physio ball) and choose the effect they like best.

11. At the end of the activity, position group members so that they have the opportunity to say goodbye to one another, either by looking at or reaching out to each other.

Variations on the method

1. Tape the material to a table top and paint as a seated group activity using hands, noses and elbows as well as brushes and rollers.

2. Painters can make individual items with smaller pieces of material, which can be pegged up or used along with a fan.

3. Use fluorescent tulle.

4. Use paper – black is effective but the paint needs to be applied more thickly.

5. Use the fluorescent paints for the title of the work and name of the person who did it, so it will also show up in the dark light.

6. Place material or paper onto wet paint on the table or floor to get a print.

7. Reduce the number of choices (colours, ways of applying paint, etc.) for painters who respond to a more structured approach.

8. Try doing the painting in the darkroom, with a painter who is already familiar with the environment and enjoys working in dark light.

Warnings!

- Use an appropriate safe procedure with blue/black light – don't allow participants to stare into the light.

- Don't use UV lamps if any participant has recently had a massage with essential oils.

- Reduce the light in the darkroom gradually so that painters are not plunged suddenly into very strange surroundings. The effect can be very powerful, especially with a large piece of work.

- Refer to the precautions listed in Appendix 14.

FOIL PAINTING/CORRUGATED CARD

Painting on different surfaces.

Aims

1. To provide a tactile experience (variety of textures/temperatures).
2. To provide an olfactory experience (variety of smells).
3. To provide a visual experience (variety of colours, tin foil).
4. To provide an interactive environment.
5. To encourage participation in an activity.
6. To provide an opportunity to express likes and dislikes.
7. To provide an opportunity to make choices.
8. To encourage participants to use a switch and teach them the concept of cause and effect.
9. To have fun.

Materials and equipment

- Detergent
- Warm water
- Tin foil
- Corrugated card
- Bubble wrap
- Tempera paints

- Large sheets of white or black paper
- Glue brush and glue
- Sponge/paint roller
- Adapted paint brushes with large handles
- Cardboard

Method

1. Position group members so that they have the opportunity to greet one another, either by looking at or reaching out to each other.
2. Pass detergent around to smell and feel.
3. Add detergent to warm water and pass around to explore.
4. Pass tin foil around to look at and listen to by scrunching up or running fingers along the foil.
5. Pass corrugated card around to feel and listen to by running fingers along the corrugations. If the card is held close to the body participants can also experience vibration from running fingers over the corrugations.
6. Pass bubble wrap around to feel and listen to by popping the bubbles.
7. Add detergent to the paints to help them stick to the different surfaces.
8. Paint on the different surfaces using hands.
9. If individuals do not like using their hands, use adapted paint brushes with large handles, or rollers.
10. Take prints from the different surfaces.
11. When mounting the prints, cut a piece of the original unprinted surface that was printed from and glue onto the print to show how the print was created.
12. Wrap foil painting around the edges of cardboard picture frames as decoration. The participants can take these picture frames away as gifts.
13. At the end of the activity, position group members so that they have the opportunity to say goodbye to one another, either by looking at or reaching out to each other.

GLITTER LEISURE DOUGH

Aims

1. To provide a tactile experience (variety of textures/consistencies/vibrations).
2. To provide an olfactory experience (variety of smells).
3. To provide an auditory experience (sounds of the electrical equipment).
4. To provide a visual experience (looking at the glitter).
5. To encourage an interactive environment.
6. To encourage participation in the activity.
7. To provide an opportunity to express likes and dislikes.
8. To provide an opportunity to make choices.
9. To encourage participants to use a switch and teach them the concept of cause and effect.
10. To have fun.

Materials and equipment

- 2 cups flour
- 2 cups water
- 3 tbsp oil
- 1 cup salt
- 2 tbsp cream of tartar
- Food colouring (e.g. green, red)
- Food essences (e.g. peppermint, strawberry)
- Glitter
- Power box
- Switches

- Electric food processor
- Bowls
- Microwave-proof bowl
- Microwave
- Garlic press
- Play dough equipment
- Trays/boards
- Bubble wrap, chicken wire, fluted cardboard, or string
- Adapted cookie cutters

Method

1. Position group members so that they have the opportunity to greet one another, either by looking at or reaching out to each other.
2. Pass around the different ingredients to feel and smell.
3. Use the electric food processor with power box and switch to mix the ingredients. Place participants' hands on the appliance or table to feel the vibrations.
4. Pour the ingredients into a microwave-proof bowl.
5. Microwave on high power for 5 minutes, stopping at intervals to stir as the mixture cooks (experiment with the time in the microwave depending on the type of appliance).
6. Pass around to feel the warm leisure dough. Add green food colouring, peppermint essence and glitter. *Check that the leisure dough is not too hot before passing it around to feel, look at and smell.*
7. Make another batch of leisure dough and add red food colouring, strawberry essence and glitter. Pass around to compare warm and cool dough.
8. Line trays/boards with bubble wrap, chicken wire, fluted cardboard, or string to make up different surfaces for participants to feel and press the dough into to get textured effects.
9. Assist participants to squeeze dough through play dough equipment to make different shapes. Press through a garlic press to make thin strings of dough.
10. Cut the dough with adapted cutters, which have thick horizontal or vertical handles.
11. At the end of the activity, position group members so that they have the opportunity to say goodbye to one another, either by looking at or reaching out to each other.

GLITTERY COLLAGE/GLITTERY MOBILE

Aims

1. To provide a tactile experience (variety of textures).
2. To provide a visual experience.
3. To provide an auditory experience (variety of sounds).
4. To encourage an interactive environment.
5. To encourage participation in the activity.
6. To provide an opportunity to express likes and dislikes.
7. To provide an opportunity to make choices.
8. To have fun.

Materials and equipment

- Large piece of paper/card
- Black paint
- Adapted paint brushes
- Sponges
- Glue
- Collection of shiny silver items (e.g. silver toffee papers, silver tinsel, silver glitter, tin foil, silver wrapping paper, wine bags, holographic paper)
- Packets beans/peas/pasta
- Bowls
- Scissors
- Water
- Silver tray
- Torch
- Tray
- String

Method

1. Position group members so that they have the opportunity to greet one another, either by looking at or reaching out to each other.
2. Paint the piece of paper/card black, using adapted paint brushes, sponges, hands/fingers. Some participants may require co-active assistance to paint.
3. Set the paper aside to dry.
4. Pass around packets of dried peas, beans and pasta to explore. Help individuals to feel the beans in the packet and listen to the sound of the packets as they are dropped onto a tray/table.
5. Open the packets and co-actively pour the beans/peas/pasta into bowls. Pass the bowls around for participants to feel the contents. Shake the bowls and listen to the noise the beans/peas/pasta make.
6. Spray the beans/peas/pasta silver and set aside to dry.
7. Pass the silver items (tinsel, foil, etc.) around to feel, scrunch and tear. Fill the wine bag with water and pass around to feel.
8. Empty the wine bag and cut into pieces.
9. Glue the silver objects onto the black paper to create a glitter collage. Alternatively, cut the black paper into smaller shapes and glue the silver objects onto these to make a mobile, using string.
10. Pass the collage/mobile around to feel.
11. Hang the mobile/pin up the collage. Turn off the lights and shine the torch onto the collage/mobile. Encourage participants to look at the effect of the light on the glittery objects.
12. At the end of the session, position group members so that they have the opportunity to say goodbye to one another, either by looking at or reaching out to each other.

HERB VINEGAR

This activity should be run over two sessions.

Aims

1. To provide a gustatory experience (variety of tastes).
2. To provide an olfactory experience (variety of smells).
3. To provide a tactile experience (variety of textures).
4. To provide an auditory experience (sound of the electrical equipment).
5. To provide a visual experience (using the UV lamp).
6. To encourage an interactive environment.
7. To encourage participation in the activity.
8. To provide an opportunity to express likes and dislikes.
9. To provide an opportunity to make choices.
10. To encourage participants to use a switch and teach them the concept of cause and effect.
11. To have fun.

Materials and equipment

- Cider vinegar or white wine vinegar
- Sprigs of mint, parsley, tarragon, chives
- Rose petals
- Cloves
- 1 lemon
- Electric grater
- Power box
- Switches

- Bowls
- Funnel
- Lightweight jug
- Bottles with lids
- Decorations (ribbon, labels, fluorescent paper)
- UV lamp

Method

Activity 1: making the vinegar

1. Position group members so that they have the opportunity to greet one another, either by looking at or reaching out to each other.
2. Co-actively pass around the herbs and rose petals for them to feel and smell.
3. Score the lemon to release the aroma, and pass around to feel and smell.
4. Using the electric grater with power box and switch, grate the lemon. Place participants' hands on the appliance or table to feel the vibrations.
5. Pass some of the lemon around to taste.
6. Offer participants a choice of herb/rose petals (they may indicate their preferences through their behaviour).
7. Fill individual bottles with chosen herbs/rose petals.
8. Put cloves in a bowl and pass around to feel.
9. Add a clove and the zest of $\frac{1}{4}$ lemon to each bottle.
10. Pass vinegar around to smell and taste.
11. Co-actively assist participants to fill bottles with the vinegar.
12. Screw on the lids and leave on a sunny windowsill for a fortnight, turning from time to time.
13. At the end of the activity, position group members so that they have the opportunity to say goodbye to one another, either by looking at or reaching out to each other.

Activity 2: rebottling and decorating the vinegar

1. Position group members so that they have the opportunity to greet one another, either by looking at or reaching out to each other.
2. Strain the matured herb vinegar into clean bottles, each containing a small sprig of the chosen herb.
3. Decorate the bottles with ribbon and/or labels. Assist participants to make their own labels. If using fluorescent paper, examine it under the UV lamp first.
4. Spend the rest of the activity exploring the different herbs and rose petals again.
5. At the end of the activity, position group members so that they have the opportunity to say goodbye to one another, either by looking at or reaching out to each other.

ICING SUGAR ART

Aims

1. To provide a tactile experience (variety of textures).
2. To provide an olfactory experience (variety of smells).
3. To provide a visual experience (variety of colours).
4. To encourage an interactive environment.
5. To encourage participation in the activity.
6. To provide an opportunity to express likes and dislikes.
7. To provide an opportunity to make choices.
8. To encourage participants to use a switch and teach them the concept of cause and effect.
9. To have fun.

Materials and equipment

- Icing sugar
- Water
- Food dye
- Food essences
- Paper
- Eyedropper
- Paint brushes
- Bowls
- Cotton wool balls

Method

1. Position group members so that they have the opportunity to greet one another, either by looking at or reaching out to each other.
2. Pass the water and icing sugar around to feel.
3. Dissolve some icing sugar in water. Experiment with different amounts of icing sugar to water.
4. Put food essences onto cotton wool balls and pass around to smell.
5. Add food essences to the sugar water to get a scented 'picture'.
6. Paint the icing sugar water onto paper, covering as much or as little of the paper as required.
7. If participants have good hand skills, assist them to drop small amounts of food dye onto the icing sugar water using an eyedropper or dab using a paint brush (with the handle adapted if necessary).
8. The food dye will 'bleed' into the icing sugar water to create interesting patterns.
9. If too much food dye is placed onto the paper or the colours are dropped too close together, the individual blots will bleed into each other. This will create a different type of pattern.
10. Leave to dry. This may take a few days, depending on how watery the icing sugar water was. (Therefore, this activity cannot be completed in one session.)
11. When the paintings are dry, cut out shapes and mount onto card.
12. At the end of the activity, position group members so that they have the opportunity to say goodbye to one another, either by looking at or reaching out to each other.

MUSIC

Aims

1. To encourage participation in a group.
2. To encourage an interactive environment.
3. To provide participants with an opportunity to listen to different types of music.
4. To provide an opportunity to make choices.
5. To build up a list of participants' likes and dislikes.
6. To encourage participants to use stereotypical movements in a purposeful way (e.g. banging table to banging a drum).
7. To have fun.

Materials and equipment

- CD or tape player
- CDs or tapes
- Box of musical instruments (e.g. bells)
- Power box
- Drums
- Switches
- Maracas/shakers
- Wind chimes
- Tambourine
- Big Mack (single message device)

Method

1. Position group members so that they have the opportunity to greet one another, either by looking at or reaching out to each other.
2. Attach the CD or tape players to the power box and switch so that participants can take turns to use it to listen to different types of music, e.g. rock, classical, pop, country. Place participants' hands on the appliance or table to feel the vibrations. Note participants' reactions.
3. Play the music loudly and softly. Do participants notice the difference and when the music stops/starts?
4. Hold the wind chimes/bells in front of and behind participants. Note whether or not they turn towards the sound. Move wind chimes/bells and note whether or not they track the sound.
5. Encourage participants to pass around the box of musical instruments and choose one.
6. Ask one participant to turn on the music and see whether or not participants can play along with the music. When the music stops, encourage participants to stop playing their instrument. Work on the concepts of stop and go.
7. If participants are unable to play the musical instruments, play the instruments for them and note their reactions. Do they prefer one type of musical instrument to another?
8. If participants indicate a preference for a musical instrument but are unable to play it, record the sound into a Big Mack (single message device) and encourage them to play the instrument through the Big Mack, or a switch attached to the Big Mack.
9. During another activity make your own musical instruments e.g. shakers, drums.
10. At the end of the activity, assist group members to replace the instruments in the box, then position them so that they have the opportunity to say goodbye to one another, either by looking at or reaching out to each other.

PEANUT BUTTER DOUGH

Aims

1. To provide a tactile experience (variety of textures).
2. To provide an olfactory experience (variety of smells).
3. To provide an interactive environment.
4. To encourage participation in the activity.
5. To provide an opportunity to express likes and dislikes.
6. To provide an opportunity to make choices.
7. To encourage participants to use a switch and teach them the concept of cause and effect.
8. To have fun.

Materials and equipment

- 1 cup peanut butter
- 1 cup powdered milk
- 1 cup honey
- 1 cup uncooked oatmeal

- Electric food processor
- Power box
- Switches
- Bowls

Method

1. Position group members so that they have the opportunity to greet one another, either by looking at or reaching out to each other.
2. Put the ingredients in bowls and pass around to smell and feel.
3. Put the ingredients in the electric food processor and, using the power box with switch, mix until smooth. Place participants' hands on the appliance or table to feel the vibrations.
4. Pass around the finished dough to feel and smell.
5. Encourage participants to push their fingers into dough, make shapes with dough, roll dough into sausages or balls.
6. At the end of the activity, position group members so that they have the opportunity to say goodbye to one another, either by looking at or reaching out to each other.

PAPIER MÂCHÉ

This activity can be carried out over a number of sessions.

Aims

1. To provide a tactile experience (variety of textures).
2. To provide an auditory experience (sounds of the electrical equipment).
3. To provide a visual experience (looking and tracking).
4. To encourage an interactive environment.
5. To encourage participation in the activity.
6. To provide an opportunity to express likes and dislikes.
7. To provide an opportunity to make choices.
8. To encourage participants to use a switch and teach them the concept of cause and effect.
9. To have fun.

Materials and equipment

Ingredients for glue
- 4¼ oz (120 g) flour
- 1½ tbsp salt
- Water
- Newspaper
- Old magazines
- Recycled paper
- Coloured paper
- White paper
- Balloons
- Bucket/trough
- Paints, felt tip pens, glitter, ribbon, tissue paper, crepe paper, feathers, flowers, leaves, etc. for decoration

- Petroleum jelly
- Electric blender
- Power box
- Switches
- Small jug
- Wooden spoon
- Brushes
- Strong cord
Pinata filling
- Popcorn, biscuits, nuts and sweets*
- Small presents (e.g. party hooter, balloons, streamers)

*Check that participants do not have allergies to nuts or any eating difficulties

Method

1. Position group members so that they have the opportunity to greet one another, either by looking at or reaching out to each other.
2. Explore the properties of the different types of paper (e.g. tear, scrunch, watch the paper float to the floor).
3. Tear paper into strips and store in the bucket/trough.
4. Co-actively assist participants to pour the flour and water into bowls, and pass around to feel.
5. Make the glue by mixing water with the flour and salt until smooth. Mix in the electric blender using power box and switch. Place participants' hands on the appliance or table to feel the vibrations. Use enough water to make a paste – not too watery, otherwise it will take too long for the paper to dry.

6. Pass balloons around to feel. Blow up balloons and gain participants' attention so that they can watch the balloons grow. Let some balloons go so that they can track them moving across the room. With others, squeeze the opening of the balloon as the air passes out to make a squeaking sound.

7. Pass petroleum jelly around to feel.

8. Cover the balloons with petroleum jelly.

9. Assist participants to dip the paper strips in the glue, or use brushes/fingers to spread glue onto the paper.

10. Cover the balloons with the glue and paper.

11. Cover the balloons in 3 or 4 layers.

12. Finally, cover the balloons with white paper and leave to dry.

13. When dry, burst the balloons and remove from the papier mâché cover.

14. Decorate the balloons.

15. The papier mâché balloons can be used for sensory environments (e.g. as planets). Alternatively, make a pinata by cutting a hole in the top of the balloon shell, filling it with small presents, popcorn, biscuits, nuts and sweets. Make two smaller holes and thread with strong cord. Decorate the pinata, then hang from the ceiling. Assist participants to take it in turns to hit the pinata until it breaks and the sweets and presents fall out.

16. Papier mâché can also be used to make trays and bowls. Instead of covering a balloon, cover the tops of dishes and bowls in paper and glue. When dry, lift the paper mâché covering off the dish or bowl, paint and decorate.

17. At the end of the activity, position group members so that they have the opportunity to say goodbye to one another, either by looking at or reaching out to each other.

RAINSTICKS AND SHAKERS

Aims

1. To provide a tactile experience (variety of textures).
2. To provide an auditory experience (variety of sounds).
3. To provide a visual experience.
4. To encourage an interactive environment.
5. To encourage participation in the activity.
6. To provide an opportunity to express likes and dislikes.
7. To provide an opportunity to make choices.
8. To have fun.

Materials and equipment

- Scissors
- Tape
- Different types of paper (e.g. fluorescent, holographic)
- Tubes, with lids if possible (e.g. potato chip tubes, tennis ball tubes, inside roll from wrapping paper, postage tubes)
- Powder paint
- Pepper shaker
- Uncooked rice
- Dried lentils
- Dried beans (e.g. butter beans)
- Dried macaroni
- Small jug
- Bowls
- Glue/glue gun
- Cardboard
- Paper
- UV lamp

Method

1. Position group members so that they have the opportunity to greet one another, either by looking at or reaching out to each other.
2. Pass around the packets of rice, macaroni, beans and pulses for participants to explore (help them to feel, drop onto their tray/table, etc.).
3. Open each packet and pour the contents into a small jug. Co-actively assist participants to pour the beans etc. into bowls and pass around to explore. Do not use with individuals who swallow small objects.
4. Pass around the tubes for everyone to explore.
5. Offer participants the choice of which tube and filling (rice, beans, etc.) they want to use.
6. If you are using an open-ended roll, make a base and tape it over one end.
7. Co-actively assist participants to pour their chosen filling into the tubes and seal at ends using the lids or cardboard.
8. Rice makes a pleasant sound for a rainstick. To slow down the movement of the rice in the rainstick, try cutting out a disc with a small hole in the middle and pushing it into the tubes. The disc should be larger than the diameter of the tube. Cut the edges of the disc so that, when it is pushed into the tube, it will form a funnel and the cut edges will fan out to hold it against the sides of the tube. Glue the cut edges to ensure that the funnel stays in place.
9. Pass around the different types of paper for participants to explore. Look at the fluorescent paper under the UV lamp to provide a more visually stimulating effect. Offer individuals a choice of paper (participants may express their choice by looking at the one they want). Decorate the tubes with the paper. If there is time, wet the paper then sprinkle dry powder paint onto it with the pepper shaker. When dry, use this paper to decorate the tubes.

10. Use as rainsticks by slowly tipping the tubes over, or as shakers by shaking the tubes. Encourage participants to experiment by listening to the sounds made by the beans, rice, macaroni and pulses – do the sounds differ? Also try making tubes using different combinations of rice, beans, pulses and macaroni.

11. Examine the finished rainsticks and shakers under the UV lamp.

12. At the end of the activity, position group members so that they have the opportunity to say goodbye to one another, either by looking at or reaching out to each other.

SOAPY PAINT

Aims

1. To provide a tactile experience (variety of textures/temperatures).
2. To provide an olfactory experience (variety of smells).
3. To provide a visual experience (variety of colours).
4. To provide an interactive environment.
5. To encourage participation in the activity.
6. To provide an opportunity to express likes and dislikes.
7. To provide an opportunity to make choices.
8. To encourage participants to use a switch and teach them the concept of cause and effect.
9. To have fun.

Materials and equipment

- Warm water
- Hot water
- Food colouring
- Soap flakes
- Containers for mixing (e.g. ice cream tubs)
- Electric whisk
- Power box
- Switches
- White and black construction paper/card
- Masking tape
- Essences/fragrances
- Cotton wool balls
- Formica table
- Combs

Method

1. Position group members so that they have the opportunity to greet one another, either by looking at or reaching out to each other.
2. Pass soap flakes around to feel and smell.
3. Dissolve some soap flakes in warm water and pass around to feel.
4. Put the essences/fragrances onto cotton wool balls and pass around to smell.
5. Pour ½ cup of hot water into a container; add soap flakes and colouring. Whisk using the electric whisk, power box and switch, until the paint has the consistency of whipped cream. Place participants' hands on the appliance or table to feel the vibrations.
6. Pass around to allow participants to feel the warm paint.
7. Assist participants to experiment by putting essences in with the paint.
8. Help participants to paint on paper or card using their hands. Alternatively, paint on the table and take a print from the table.
9. Make up another batch of paint, but keep it white and paint on black card.
10. Assist individuals to pull combs though the paint for a different effect.
11. At the end of the activity, position group members so that they have the opportunity to say goodbye to one another, either by looking at or reaching out to each other.

WARM CORNFLOUR FINGER PAINT

Aims

1. To provide a tactile experience (variety of textures).
2. To provide an olfactory experience (variety of smells).
3. To provide an interactive environment.
4. To provide a relaxing environment.
5. To encourage participation in an activity.
6. To provide an opportunity to express likes and dislikes.
7. To provide an opportunity to make choices.
8. To encourage participants to use a switch and teach them the concept of cause and effect.
9. To have fun.

Materials and equipment

Water ratio: 3 parts water to 1 part cornflour

- Cornflour
- Food colouring/paint
- Food essences
- Glycerine
- Soap flakes (optional)
- Electric frying pan
- Bowls
- Cotton wool balls
- Smooth paper
- Masking tape
- Wooden spoon

Method

1. Position group members so that they have the opportunity to greet one another, either by looking at or reaching out to each other.
2. Put water, cornflour, soap flakes and glycerine in bowls and pass around for participants to feel.
3. Boil 3 parts water in the electric frying pan.
4. Dissolve 1 part cornflour with cold water.
5. Add to the boiling water, stirring constantly.
6. Boil for about 1 minute until clear and thick.
7. Put drops of food essences on the cotton wool balls and pass around for participants to smell.
8. Add food colouring or paint and essences to the cornflour mixture.
9. Pass some warm mixture around for participants to look at while you make up another colour.
10. A tablespoon of glycerine may be added to make it glossy.
11. Half a cup of soap flakes may be added to give the finger paint a lumpy texture.
12. Stick the paper to a table with masking tape.
13. Place the paint onto the paper and encourage participants to use hands or feet to paint with.
14. Make this a relaxing activity by using the warm cornflour paint, playing relaxing music and using an aromatherapy diffuser to release the smell of lavender in the room.
15. At the end of the activity, position group members so that they have the opportunity to say goodbye to one another, either by looking at or reaching out to each other.

WRAPPING PAPER

This activity requires someone to be able to use an iron. If there is anyone in the group that cannot use an iron, they can still participate by exploring the sensory properties of all the materials. A support worker may then have to do the ironing.

You can extend this activity by making your own potpourri (see p.158) or pressed flowers.

Aims

1. To provide a tactile experience (variety of textures).
2. To provide an olfactory experience (variety of smells).
3. To provide an auditory the experience (sound materials make when scrunched).
4. To provide a visual experience (looking at the sequins, tinsel).
5. To encourage an interactive environment.
6. To encourage participation in the activity.
7. To provide an opportunity to express likes and dislikes.
8. To provide an opportunity to make choices.
9. To have fun.

Materials and equipment

- Waxed lunch paper (using unbleached wrapping paper gives an aged look)
- Potpourri
- Pressed flowers
- Tinsel
- Sequins

Method

1. Position group members so that they have the opportunity to greet one another, either by looking at or reaching out to each other.
2. Pass around materials to feel, smell, scrunch and listen to as appropriate.
3. Tear off a piece of waxed lunch paper about 2 ft (60 cm) long.
4. Place the paper on the table with greased side up.
5. Place either sequins, tinsel, pressed flowers or potpourri on the paper either in a random pattern or space out the materials in a pattern of participants' choice.
6. Place another piece of paper the same length on top, with the greased side down.
7. Iron the 2 pieces of waxed paper together to bond the materials inside.
8. Leave to cool slightly then pass around to feel the hot paper.
9. At the end of the activity, position group members so that they have the opportunity to say goodbye to one another, either by looking at or reaching out to each other.

YOGHURT PAINTING

Aims

1. To provide a tactile experience (variety of textures/temperatures).
2. To provide an olfactory experience (variety of smells).
3. To provide a visual experience (variety of colours).
4. To provide an interactive environment.
5. To encourage participation in the activity.
6. To provide an opportunity to express likes and dislikes.
7. To provide an opportunity to make choices.
8. To encourage participants to use a switch and teach them the concept of cause and effect.
9. To have fun.

Materials and equipment

- 3 large pots of cold plain yoghurt (as a variation use condensed milk)
- 3 food colourings
- 3 food essences to go with the colourings (e.g. strawberry for red, lemon for yellow, peppermint for green)
- Paper/card
- Masking tape
- Formica tables (so that participants can either paint directly onto the paper or paint on the table and take a print)
- Spoons
- Cotton wool balls
- Washing line
- Pegs

Method

1. Position group members so that they have the opportunity to greet one another, either by looking at or reaching out to each other.
2. Pass cold pots of yoghurt around to feel.
3. Put 1 colour in each of the yoghurt pots and mix using a spoon.
4. Put essences onto cotton wool balls and pass around to smell.
5. Add essences to the coloured pots of yoghurt as appropriate.
6. Assist participants to paint using their hands, onto paper or directly onto the table.
7. Take prints from the table.
8. Leave prints/paintings to dry and use to make cards.
9. As a variation, mix the essences and colours with condensed milk. Put paper under washing line and peg the condensed milk painting onto the line. The condensed milk will drip onto the paper below and create balls of textured 'paint'.
10. The condensed milk can also be used to cover egg-shaped pieces of card, which can then be used in an Easter activity.
11. At the end of the activity, position group members so that they have the opportunity to say goodbye to one another, either by looking at or reaching out to each other.

APPENDICES

Appendix I

Engagement background questionnaire

Person's name: _____

Questionnaire date: _____

Completed by: _____

Relationship to person: _____

Introduction

This questionnaire has been devised to gather information on people's engagement behaviours. It should be completed by one who has known the person long enough in order to be familiar with his or her behaviours.

Consider the statements in each of the sections and tick the appropriate space according to your personal judgement of the person's behaviours.

There is a choice between three responses for each statement. Please be sure to fill in only one space for a response.

Please read the brief definitions of the response categories provided below before filling in the questionnaire.

All completed questionnaires will be treated with absolute confidentiality.

Definitions of response choices	
YES	This statement is fairly typical of the person and occurs often during the day
NO	This statement is not at all typical of the person and does not occur during the day
SOMETIMES	This statement is not typical of the person but occurs sporadically or some of the time

This questionnaire was devised by Karen Bunning (speech and language therapist, UK) and has been adapted by Susan Fowler (occupational therapist), October 1999.

Section A: Self-engagement behaviours

Descriptive statement	Yes	No	Sometimes	Sensory system
Person walks in ritualistic patterns, repetitively				
Person engages in rocking behaviour				
Person bounces up and down repetitively on feet or seat				
Person spins self around repetitively while standing				
Person sways head from side to side, repetitively				
Person performs ritualistic hand and arm gestures				
Person flicks fingers in front of eyes and face, repetitively				
Person picks up scraps from floor and other surfaces				
Person manipulates objects in ritualistic way (e.g. spinning, twiddling)				
Person manipulates own clothing, repetitively				
Person touches self, repetitively				
Person utters bizarre, irrelevant verbalisations				
Person emits screams, not obviously related to distress				
Person makes repetitive non-speech sounds				
Person engages in anal/oral behaviour inappropriately				
Person masturbates in inappropriate/public places				
Person engages in self-injurious behaviour				

Section B: Person engagement behaviours

Descriptive statement	Yes	No	Sometimes
Person reacts to name being called (e.g. turns head, opens eyes, smiles) (specify)			
Person gives eye contact			
Person looks at others momentarily			
Person looks closely at another person's face			
Person watches you/tracks you moving around the room			
Person reacts to others offering hand in greeting (e.g. ignores, looks, pulls self away, reaches out) (specify)			
Person reacts to being touched in greeting (e.g. tolerates touch, shakes hands, smiles, pulls hand away, becomes agitated) (specify)			
Person changes vocalisations when greeted (e.g. becomes quiet, vocalisations increase) (specify)			
Person initiates contact (e.g. reaches for/touches in social contact)			
Person tries to get your attention in other ways (e.g. calls out, bangs the table) (specify)			
Person responds to a command (e.g. give me)			
Person imitates the actions of another person (e.g. waves goodbye) (specify)			

Section C: Object engagement behaviours

Descriptive statement	Yes	No	Sometimes
Person attends to an object			
Person tracks object			
Person watches objects near and/or far (specify)			
Person holds/explores object when placed in hand			
Person actively explores objects (e.g. mouth/lick, shake, throw, drop, hold, manipulate, visually inspect, listen to) (specify)			
Person reaches to touch objects			
Person picks up objects without prompting			
Person uses object purposefully and functionally			
Person vocalises when given an object			
Person vocalises when drops/loses an object			
Person attends to object for less than 30 seconds			
Person attends to object for more than 30 seconds (specify)			
Person has preferred object(s) (specify)			
Person makes choices between two/more objects			
Person indicates like/dislike (specify object)			

Section D: Person–object engagement behaviours

Descriptive statement	Yes	No	Sometimes
Person looks between another person and object			
Person uses an object to get a need met (e.g. holds up cup for a drink)			
Person co-actively passes an object to another person			
Person gives object to another person independently			
Person joins in activity with another person			
Person shows activity or object to another person			
Person indicates to person a desired object/activity			

Sensory assessment

Name: _____

Dates: _____

Names of assessors: _____

Self-engagement

Stimulus: Natural environment (no stimuli presented)
Response: Describe what people are doing:

Stimulus: Self-engagement behaviours
Response: What appears to cause self-engagement behaviour?
Response: What appears to cause self-engagement behaviour to stop?

Stimulus: Self-injurious behaviours
Response: What appears to cause self-injurious behaviour?
Response: What appears to cause self-injurious behaviour to stop?

Person engagement (greetings)

Stimulus: Reaction to door opening

Response:

Stimulus: Gave eye contact

Response:

Stimulus: Reaction to name spoken

Response:

Stimulus: Reaction to another name

Response:

Stimulus: Allowed hand/arm to be touched

Response:

Stimulus: Reached out – initiated interaction

Response:

Stimulus: Watched other people with interest

Response:

Stimulus: Reaction to familiar/unfamiliar people

Response:

Object engagement

Visual

Most of these stimuli can be assessed in the multisensory room.

Observe for any...
Squints:
Nystagmus:
Eye squinting:
Eye preference:
Compensatory head tilt:
Pupillary response to light:
No blink response – protective reflex:

If any of the above are observed, refer to ophthalmologist for further assessment.

Stimulus: Fixes on lights/objects? Which light/object?

Response:

Stimulus: Tracks lights/objects? Which light/object?

Response:

Stimulus: Visual field preference (two objects/lights)

Response:

Stimulus: Torch light

Response: Still/moving

Response: Near/far

Response: Central vision

Response: Peripheral vision. Lights/objects

Stimulus: Different-coloured lights

Response:

Stimulus: Fibre-optic spray

Response:

Stimulus: Hurricane tube

Response:

Stimulus: Slides

Response:

Stimulus: Light on foil/travelling lights

Response:

Stimulus: Mirror ball

Response:

Stimulus: Slinky

Response:

Stimulus: Reflection in mirror

Response:

Stimulus: Bubbles

Response:

Stimulus: Sparklers (assess outside multisensory room)

Response:

Stimulus: Visual interest in everyday objects, e.g. cup (assess during drinks/ meal times)

Response:

Movement and vibration

Stimulus: Trampoline

Response:

Stimulus: Swimming

Response:

Stimulus: Horse riding

Response:

Stimulus: Wheelchair dancing

Response:

Stimulus: Executive swivel chair

Response:

Stimulus: Being on the hydraulic van lift

Response:

Stimulus: Big fan

Response:

Stimulus: Mini-fan

Response:

Stimulus: Mini-vibrator

Response:

Stimulus: Vibrating snake

Response:

Stimulus: Vibrating spider

Response:

✓

Tactile

Assess during group activity (e.g. massage, craft group or cookery).

Stimulus: Cold objects, e.g. ice, frozen peas (wrapped in a flannel, bag), ice cream, cold water

Response:

Stimulus: Hot objects, e.g. hot pack, warm water, hot water bottle

Response:

Stimulus: Slippery objects, e.g. gak, slime, jelly

Response:

Stimulus: Hard objects, e.g. macaroni, rice, pasta, executive toy (pin man), glass/plastic bottle

Response:

Stimulus: Gritty/rough objects, e.g. gravel, sand, scourer, pine cone, rubber scrub mitt, loofah

Response:

Stimulus: Smooth objects, e.g. velvet, silk

Response:

Stimulus: Soft objects, e.g. talc, cornflour, lambswool, bubble wrap, fur, shaving foam, koosh ball

Response:

Stimulus: Sticky objects, e.g. jam, honey

Response:

Stimulus: Massage

Response:

Auditory

Some of these may be assessed during activities (e.g. music).

Stimulus: Spinning tops (also visual stimulus)

Response:

Stimulus: Bells

Response:

Stimulus: Door bell

Response:

Stimulus: Wind chimes

Response:

Stimulus: CD or tape player (music)

Response: Central vision

Stimulus: Different types of music

Response:

Stimulus: Musical instruments

Response:

Stimulus: Big Macks (large, switch-operated single message device). Quiet/loud

Response:

Stimulus: Drum (loud)

Response:

Stimulus: Beeper (loud)

Response:

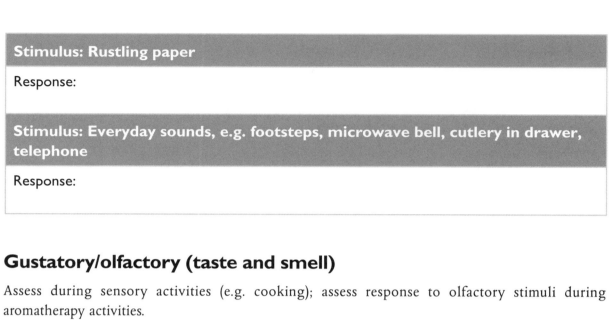

Stimulus: Rustling paper
Response:

Stimulus: Everyday sounds, e.g. footsteps, microwave bell, cutlery in drawer, telephone
Response:

Gustatory/olfactory (taste and smell)

Assess during sensory activities (e.g. cooking); assess response to olfactory stimuli during aromatherapy activities.

Stimulus: Bitter, e.g. lemon, grapefruit
Response:

Stimulus: Sugar/sweet, e.g. honey, chocolate
Response:

Stimulus: Savoury, e.g. yeast extract
Response:

Stimulus: Spicy/hot, e.g. curry powder
Response:

Stimulus: Salty, e.g. anchovies, olives
Response:

Stimulus: Strong tastes, e.g. garlic, onions, blue cheese
Response:

Stimulus: Soft textures, e.g. yoghurt
Response:

Stimulus: Hard textures, e.g. apples
Response:

Stimulus: Smell of perfume
Response:

Stimulus: Aromatherapy oils, e.g. lavender, orange, eucalyptus
Response:

Cognitive skills

Has object permanence

Demonstrated understanding of cause and effect

Was a choice made or preference indicated? How?

Attention span for different objects

Attention span for different activities

Mood

Dominant mood before the assessment
Dominant mood during the assessment
Mood change

Position assessed in

Wheelchair
Lying on back
Lying over wedge
Lying on side
Sitting on floor
Other
Best functional position

Sensory assessment – additional information

This appendix sets out definitions and also additional information on how people respond to different stimuli and how they use objects.

Observation of reaction to stimuli

When presenting different stimuli, observe people's responses to them.
Observe changes in activity levels of:

- head
- face
- mouth
- eyes
- hands
- arms
- legs
- body
- vocalisations.

Definitions for eye conditions

- Squints: deviation in position of the eye.
- Nystagmus: rhythmic involuntary movement of the eyeball.
- Hippus: small constrictions/dilations of pupil, spontaneous movements of iris not due to outside stimulus (e.g. light).
- Eye squinting: facial expression indicates trying to see (e.g. eyes half closed, eyes screwed up).
- Eye preference: cover one eye, show light/object.

Testing to see whether or not a person can see an object if they do not appear to see objects

A crude test to see if a person can see an object is to pair a bright object with a puff of air. Set up a routine, where you show the object and then squeeze a bottle to puff wind onto the face. After a time, the person may blink or move in response to the object, anticipating the puff of air.

Observation of people interacting with objects

Observe what a person does with an object. For example:

- looks

- tracks

- reaches for

- manipulates

- holds

- throws/drops

- passes to you.

Mood change

Note what kind of mood people are during the session (e.g. alert, happy, asleep, agitated). Also note whether their mood changes during the session and why you think it changed (e.g. the person may arrive very agitated but quiet music may calm them down; they may be very sleepy but bright lights arouse them).

Object permanence

When a person realises that an object still exists, even if they cannot see it.

Cause and effect

When a person realises that when they do something (e.g. press a switch) it causes something else to happen (e.g. the light comes on).

Definitions of cognitive levels

The following definitions are from Coupe O'Kane and Goldbart (1998)/Bloomberg and West (1997).

Reflexive

- May sleep a lot.

- Reflex activity – sucking/grasping.

- Startles with touch/loud noises.

- Vocalises discomfort/distress.

- Watches people/objects momentarily.

Reactive

- Changes in behaviour occur when presented with people/objects (e.g. increased movement of head, smiling, vocalising – may mean likes something, but carer interprets behaviour).

- Reacts to different tones of voice, facial expression, body language.

- Does not initiate interactions but reacts to them.

- Responds to consistent routines – can anticipate (e.g. see cup/feels it against lip and opens mouth).

- Shared attention – individual appears to look at same object.

- Looks and turns to sound – particularly voices.

Proactive

- Reaches out to explore environment rather than being presented with objects.

- Functional objects have meaning (e.g. cup means drink).

- Reacts differently to strangers and familiar people.

- Repeats movements that caused interesting things to happen.

- Uses objects in different ways (e.g. shake, bang, throw).

- Has consistent response that can be moulded to mean 'more' (e.g. vocalises when given eye contact and asked 'Do you want some more?', e.g. food); at this stage individuals may not realise the meaning is 'more' and may use the same vocalisation for 'yes' (e.g. 'May I take your bag off the tray?').

- Reaches for objects – carer interprets as choice.

The following definitions are from Knickerbocker (1980)/Sanderson and Gitsham (1990).

Avoid

- Very passive/asleep.

- Pulls away from people/from touching things.

- Turns away from people/the table.

- Takes self away from group and crouches in the corner.

- Activities presented to the person rather than person reaching out to explore independently.

- May avoid touch/find it irritating.

✓

Explore

- Accepts touch from familiar people they can trust – their behaviours are predictable (people know they are free to withdraw whenever they want).

- May start touching everything.

- Reaches out to explore surroundings.

- Develops preferences.

- Repeats actions that produced interesting results.

- Begins to understand cause and effect – initially, I do something and something happens, but they don't link the two events, and moving onto when I do something, something happens but I'm not sure how it happened.

Organise

- Understands cause and effect – when I do this, that happens.

- Understands object permanence.

- Discriminates between different stimuli – recognises things that are similar and things that are different.

Integrate

- Uses all senses to explore environment.

- Integrates the senses (e.g. has hand–eye coordination).

- Integrates past experiences with present (e.g. I felt that before and liked it).

- Experiments with different actions on the same object, and the same action on different objects.

- Uses trial and error when exploring objects and seeing how they work/ sounds they make.

Conceptualise

- Problem-solving skills.

- No longer trial and error.

Self-engagement behaviours

More detailed form

Name	Self-engagement behaviour				The sense(s) being stimulated				
	What is the behaviour?	Non-functional?	Repetitive?	Self-stimulating?	Sight	Hearing	Taste/smell	Touch	Movement

Basic form

Name	Self-engagement behaviour	The sense(s) being stimulated

Self-engagement analysis

Name: _____   **Date:** _____

Self-engagement behaviour (e.g. rocking)	What system does this stimulate? (e.g. vestibular)	What causes self-engagement to stop? (e.g. trampoline)	What system does this stimulate? (e.g. vestibular)	Activity ideas (e.g. sessions on the trampoline)

Interest chart

Individual's name: _____

Date: _____

Name of assessor: _____

Assessment based on: (please circle)

               Own knowledge   Interview   Observation

If based on interview, name of person interviewed: _____

Relationship to individual: _____

Environment	Objects often used and likes	Activities person often does and enjoys	People individual is often with and likes to be with
Home			
Work or day centre			
Leisure time			

Appendix 5

Engagement checklist

Name: _____   **Date:** _____

Self-engagement behaviours	Person engagement behaviours	Object engagement behaviours	Other comments

Likes and dislikes form

Likes	What sensory system do these stimulate?	Dislikes	What sensory system do these stimulate?

Personal communication dictionary form

Personal communication dictionary for: _____

What _____ does (describe behaviours, when, where and what occurs)	What this might mean (interpret the behaviour)	What you should do (how communication partner should respond)

People involved in completing this form: _____

_____

Date commenced: _____

Sensory assessment summary form

Name:	Date:
How likes are indicated	**How dislikes are indicated**
For more information refer to personal communication dictionary sheet	
Things liked	**Things disliked**
For more information refer to separate likes and dislikes sheet	
Any self-engagement behaviours? How to stop/reduce them	
Interested in people – how do you know?	
Interested in objects – how do you know?	
Any person–object engagement? (Need both to be functional)	

Which sensory system do people appear to be using most? (Circle)

Visual	Gustatory	Olfactory
Auditory	Tactile	Vestibular

Level of communication

Unintentional communication	Informal intentional
· Reflexive	
· Reactive	
· Proactive	

Cognitive level (Circle)

Avoid	Integrate	Organise
Explore	Conceptualise	

Recommendations

Include:

· activity ideas

· types of activities people enjoy

· individual skill development programmes (e.g. switching programmes)

· how to increase independence (e.g. at meal times)

· how to set up the environment for communication (e.g. develop 'more' response and choice making)

· information on techniques (e.g. how to massage).

Example of a multisensory room recording form

Please tick which pieces of equipment you used and whether or not the equipment was working. If equipment is not working, please inform _____ or fill in faults book kept _____

Name:	Date:

Multisensory room

Describe what people are doing and their mood when they first enter the room

Position in multisensory room (Circle)

Wheelchair	Lying on back	Lying on front over wedge
Lying on side	Sitting on floor	Other

Self-engagement behaviours

Describe:

What appears to cause self-engagement behaviour to stop?

Self-injurious behaviours

Describe:

What appears to cause self-injurious behaviour?

Mood change

Describe whether a person's mood changes (e.g. arrived agitated, but became calm, became agitated when a certain piece of equipment came in)

How long did it take for the person to become calm?

How long did it take for the person to stop self-engagement behaviours/self-injurious behaviours?

Person engagement

Gave eye contact:

Allowed hand/arm to be touched:

Reached out – initiated interaction:

Demonstrated shared attention (e.g. looked at you and looked at a piece of equipment):

Object engagement

Note attention span for different objects. Note if used switch I (independent), C (co-active).

Reaction to:

· Fibreoptic spray

· Slides

· Mirror ball/spotlight and colour wheel

· Hurricane tube

· Odyessy light/lights on foil/spinning tops/magic lights

· Fan/wind chimes/bells/curtains/streamers

· Vibrating snake

· Cassette recorder/Big Macks (quiet/loud)

· Pethna (music box)

· Other

How was a choice made or preference indicated?

Length of session

Useful equipment for sensory activities

Electric tin opener

Electric knife

Electric whisk

Electric food processor/blender

Electric coffee/nut grinder

Electric juicer

Electric frying pan

Swirl Art (from toy shops); this can be switch-adapted and also used as a switch dice

Switch-operated water pourer

Power boxes/power links

Switches

Small lightweight jug

UV lamp

Adapted paint brushes/rollers/stamps (as illustrated)

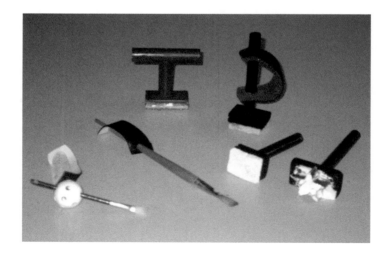

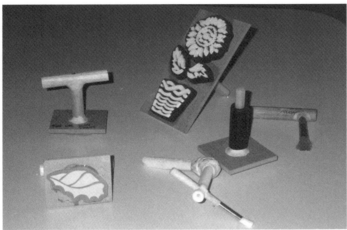

Adapted cookie cutters (as illustrated)

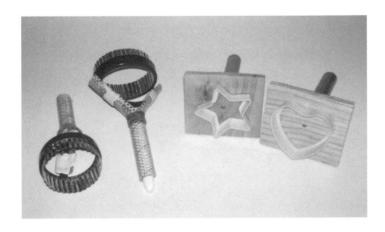

✓

Equipment commonly found in multisensory rooms

Tactile

Vibro-acoustic beanbags
Vibrating beds
Vibrating mats
Massage tubes/snakes
Ball pool
Tactile walls
Activity walls
Fan
Mats, chairs, beanbags, beds

Movement

Leaf chair
Hammock
Bubble tube
Waterbed or water chair

Visual

Bubble tube
Solar projector
Mirrors
Spotlight and colour wheel
Mirror ball
Fibre-optic spray
Hurricane tube
Slide projector
Fairy lights
UV lamp/UV corner
Infinity tunnel
Catherine wheel
Ladder lights

Hearing

Sound system
Musical walls or floors
Soundbeam
Echo tubes
Wind chimes

Smell

Aroma diffuser
Smell tubes

Other

Integrated switching system or power boxes
Switches:

- wireless switches

- sound switch

- jelly bean switch

- Big Red

- Buddy Button

- Big Mack (one-message communication device).

Companies that supply multisensory equipment

Abilitations Multisensory

3155 Northwoods Pkwy
Norcross, GA 30071
USA
Customer service, toll free, tel: 001 800 850 8603
International fax: 001 770 263 0897
Evan Siegel: 001 800 444 5700 (ext. 7295)
Email: esiegel@sportime.com
Website: www.abilitations.com

Flaghouse Inc.

601 Flaghouse Drive
Hasbrouck Heights, NJ 07604-3116
USA
Tel: 001 800 793 7900
Fax: 001 800 793 7922
Website: www.flaghouse.com

Indomed Pty Ltd

41 Forsyth St
O'Connor, WA 6163
Australia
Tel: 0061 (08) 9331 6711
Freecall: 0061 1800 884 634
Fax: 0061 (08) 9331 6722
Email: info@indomed.com.au
Website: www.indomed.com

Mike Ayres Design and Development Ltd

The Paddocks
Dore
Sheffield S17 3LD
UK
Tel: 0044 (0) 114 235 6880
Fax: 0044 (0) 114 235 6881
Email: enquiry@mike-ayres.co.uk
Website: www.mike-ayres.co.uk

ROMPA®

Goyt Side Road
Chesterfield
Derbyshire S40 2PH
UK
Tel: 0044 (0) 1246 211777
Fax: 0044 (0) 1246 221802
Website: www.rompa.com

Sensco Multisensory Environments

114 Bentinck House
Bentinck Street
Ashton OL6 7SZ
UK
Tel: 0044 (0) 161 343 8823
Email: enquiries@sensco.co.uk
Website: www.sensco.co.uk

Sensory Fun and Learning – Australia

6 Rupert Road
Warburton
Victoria 3799
Australia
Tel: 0061 (03) 5966 2208
Email: sfandl@optusnet.com.au

Sensory Plus
(Part of Kirton Healthcare Group)

23 Rookwood Way
Haverhill
Suffolk CB9 8PB
UK
Freephone: 0044 (0) 800 212709
Tel: 0044 (0) 1440 705352
Fax: 0044 (0)1440 706199
Email: enquiries@sensoryplus.co.uk
Website: www.sensoryplus.co.uk

Spacecraft Ltd

Titus House
29 Saltaire Road
Shipley
West Yorkshire BD18 3HH
UK
Tel: 0044 (0) 1274 581007
Fax: 0044 (0) 1274 531966
Website: www.spacekraft.co.uk

Technical Solutions
109 Ferndale Road
Silvan
3795 Victoria
Australia
Tel: 0061 (03) 9737 9000
Fax: 0061 (03) 9737 9111
Email: inquire@tecsol.com.au
Website: www.tecsol.com.au
(Will also switch-adapt equipment)

TFH Special Needs Toys
5–7 Severnside Business Park
Severn Road
Stourport-on-Severn
Worcestershire DY13 9HT
UK
Tel: 0044 (0) 1299 827820
Fax: 0044 (0) 1299 827035
Website: www.tfhuk.com

The Sensory Company International Ltd
Broad Lane Business Centre
Westfield Lane
South Elmsall WF9 2JX
UK
Tel: 0044 (0) 845 838 2233
Fax: 0044 (0) 845 838 2234
Email: webinfo@thesensorycompany.co.uk
Website: www.thesensorycompany.co.uk/

Wilkins International Pty Ltd
(Agents for Spacekraft in Australia)
Unit 14
173–181 Rooks Road
Vermont, VIC 3133
Australia
Tel: 0061 (03) 9874 1033
Fax: 0061 (03) 9874 6611
Email: wilkins@wilkinsinternational.com.au

The benefits of and the skills required to run sensory-focused activities

Benefits of using a sensory-focused approach	Skills required to provide sensory-focused activities
Increased interaction with support people and peers	Good observational skills
Increased participation in activities	Good interaction skills
Increased communication (e.g. increased eye contact, vocalisations, greater understanding of people's body language)	Ability to communicate with unintentional communicators
Reduction in self-engagement behaviours	Being consistent
Environment set up for choice making and people making more choices	Being a facilitator rather than a 'doer'
Increased awareness of environment and other people	Giving people time to respond
Increased self-esteem	Being patient
Increased responses to people and objects	Having enthusiasm
Increased initiation	Giving encouragement
Increase in turn-taking	Respecting people
People have fun and enjoy themselves	Being aware of people's needs and how they express them
Increase of skills (e.g. using a switch)	Setting realistic goals – don't try to do too much during an activity
Increase understanding of likes, dislikes and interests, and how people express preferences	Problem-solving skills
	Being flexible
	Giving yourselves enough time to prepare for activities
	Good recording skills – writing down what you observe and what you think it means
	Having a vision

Precautions when using UV light

1. Do not look directly into the light – angle the lamp down or build a pelmet around the UV light tube.

2. Do not use after a massage with certain essential oils (e.g. bergamot) as this makes the skin more sensitive to UV light and can cause a sunburn effect. Check with an aromatherapist before using essential oils.

3. Some drugs will also make people more sensitive to the UV light – check participants' medication and precautions.

4. There seems to be little consensus on what is considered safe. As a rule, use only for 30 minutes at a time, or if your eyes feel 'flickery' or you are getting a headache, have shorter sessions. Support people are more likely to be exposed to the UV for longer than the people with whom they are working, especially if carrying out consecutive assessments.

5. Flo Longhorn quotes research from Dr Brian Duffey, who gives the example of 'a teacher and pupil working for two hours in a dark room, approximately four feet (1.2 metres) from the light source. This would result in a dose of ultraviolet radiation equivalent to about 48 seconds of summer sunshine. He concludes that, if UV light is used appropriately in darkrooms, then there is no risk to the eyes or skin' (Longhorn 1997, p.5).

6. When replacing a light tube, remember to use a blue-black one, which looks purple when it is turned off. Do not use the ones that look white as these are for sunbeds. They do not cause objects to fluoresce and are hazardous to use in a multisensory room.

7. Be aware that some people may feel threatened or claustrophobic in dark spaces.

Glossary

Big Mack
A large, switch-operated single-message device. It can record single messages or sounds (e.g. the telephone).

Co-active assistance
A method of assisting individuals to participate in an activity or explore an object. The support worker moves the individual's body part (e.g. arm) so that they can experience the movement associated with operating equipment or exploring an object. One method of co-active assistance is when the support worker supports the other person's hand and elbow. In this way, the support worker can assist the other person to reach forward to press a switch, feel an object or use an object functionally (e.g. pour milk from a jug).

Complex communication needs
Having little or no speech. Balandin (2002) has described this as follows:

> People with Complex Communication Needs have communication problems associated with a wide range of physical, sensory and environmental causes which restrict/limit their ability to participate independently in society. They and their communication partners may benefit from using augmentative and alternative communication (AAC) methods either temporarily or permanently.

Intensive interaction
Intensive interaction describes a way of communicating with people with profound and multiple disabilities. It is based on the interaction style that a parent has with a young baby and the focus is on the process of interaction rather than its outcome.

Multisensory room
Multisensory rooms are designated rooms containing many pieces of equipment, mainly those that stimulate the visual and auditory senses. A list of equipment that is commonly found in multisensory rooms can be found in Appendix 11, and a list of companies that supply multisensory equipment in Appendix 12.

Multisensory rooms grew out of the 'snoezelen™' concept, which was developed in Holland (Hulsegge and Verheul 1987). The term is a contraction of two Dutch words meaning 'sniffing' and 'dozing' and is meant to convey the feeling of activity (as in sniffing) with relaxation (dozing). Originally it was a very nebulous concept and was applied to any activity that stimulated the senses in an attractive environment. However, over time, the term was used in a more restricted sense so that snoezelen™ rooms were developed. The multisensory room developed out of these snoezelen™ rooms, which were designed mainly for relaxation, while multisensory rooms themselves have a broader application, including assessment and skills training.

Object engagement

Any behaviour where the person engages with an object in a purposeful way (e.g. looking at, tracking, reaching for, holding and using the object in a functional way).

Object symbol

An object or partial object used to represent an activity. This is used as a cue to alert people to an activity that is about to occur.

Person engagement

Any behaviours where the person engages with another person (e.g. making eye contact, watching a person moving around the room, reaching out to a person, vocalising at and smiling at another person).

Person–object engagement

Any behaviour where the person engages with an object and person at the same time (e.g. looking at a person and an object – shared attention – giving an object to a person).

Power box

A piece of equipment used to make any electrical appliance switch-accessible. External switches are plugged into the power box, which allows people with disabilities to operate appliances without the need for good fine motor skills.

Self-engagement behaviour

Any behaviours that are non-purposeful, often repetitive and self-stimulating (e.g. rocking, finger flicking). The term self-engagement has been used in preference to self-stimulation as some of these behaviours may originally have been self-stimulating but are now just habits. The person engages with the 'self' during self-engagement behaviours and needs to be encouraged to interact with their environment instead, engaging with other people and objects.

If objects are used in a repetitive, non-purposeful way (e.g. twirling shoelaces), then this is self-engagement behaviour, not object engagement.

Sensory defensiveness

Wilbarger and Wilbarger (1991) have described this as follows:

> A tendency to react negatively or with alarm to sensory input that is generally considered harmless or non-irritating is typical of sensory defensiveness. Common symptoms may include over sensitivity to light or unexpected touch, sudden movement or over reaction to unstable surfaces, high frequency noises, excesses of noise or visual stimuli and certain smells.

Sensory profile

A way of describing each person's unique sensory needs. For example, some people may easily be overstimulated and others may need more stimulation to take notice of the things around them.

The sensory profile (Dunn 1999a, 1999b) is an evaluation tool that poses a number of questions in relation to behavioural responses to everyday sensory experiences.

Shared attention

Part of person–object engagement behaviour, where two people each alternate their gaze between a person and an object. Both of them therefore attend to the same object or event. Each individual is sharing an activity with another person.

Skills enhancement unit

An example of a sensory-focused programme. It provides the opportunity for people who have physical and multiple disabilities to develop specific skills through participation in an intensive group programme for a predetermined length of time.

The unit also has a support person training component, where they can learn how to choose and present activities to enable people with disabilities to further develop their skills and maximise participation.

Unintentional communication

A level of communication where support people allocate meaning to a person's behaviour.

References

Barber, M. (1994) 'Contingency awareness: putting research into the classroom.' In J. Coupe O'Kane and B. Smith (eds) *Taking Control – Enabling People with Learning Difficulties.* London: David Fulton.

Bloomberg, K. (1996) *prAACtically speaking – Functional Communication Strategies*, information and resource booklet. Victoria: ComTec: Disability Communication and Technology Solutions.

Bloomberg, K. and West, D. (1997) *PICTURE IT Partners in Communication Training Using Real Environments*, interactive teaching CRC. Victoria: Scope (Vic.) Ltd.

Bloomberg, K. and West, D. (1999) *The Triple C Checklist of Communication Competencies*, assessment manual CRC. Victoria: Scope (Vic.) Ltd.

Brown, C. (2001) 'What is the best environment for me?' *Occupational Therapy in Mental Health 17*, 3/4, 115–125.

Brown, C. and Dunn, W. (2002) *The Adult Sensory Profile.* San Antonio, TX: Psychological Corporation.

Bunning, K. (1996) *Development of an 'Individualised Sensory Environment' for Adults with Learning Disabilities and an Evaluation of its Effects on their Interactive Behaviours.* Unpublished thesis, City University, London.

Cermak, S.A. and Daunhaur, L.A. (1997) 'Sensory processing in the postinstitutionalized child.' *American Journal of Occupational Therapy 51*, 7, 500–507.

Coupe O'Kane, J. and Goldbart, J. (1998) *Communication Before Speech* (2nd edn). London: David Fulton.

Dunn, W. (1999a) *The Sensory Profile.* San Antonio, TX: Psychological Corporation.

Dunn, W. (1999b) *The Sensory Profile Manual.* San Antonio, TX: Psychological Corporation.

Dunn, W. (2001) 'The sensations of everyday life: theoretical, conceptual and pragmatic considerations.' *American Journal of Occupational Therapy 55*, 6, 608–620.

Dunn, W. (2002) *The Infant Toddler Sensory Profile.* San Antonio, TX: Psychological Corporation.

Firth, G. (2004) *A Framework for Recognising Attainment in Intensive Interaction.* Leeds: Mental Health NHS Trust.

Glenn, S. (1987) 'Interactive Approaches to Working with Children with Profound and Multiple Learning Difficulties.' Paper from conference on Interactive Approaches to the Education of Children with Severe Learning Difficulties, 10–12 April 1987, Westhill College, Birmingham, UK.

Hulsegge, J. and Verheul, A. (1987) *Snoezelen: Another World.* Chesterfield: ROMPA UK.

Hutchinson, R. (ed.) (1991) 'The Whittington Hall Project – A Report from Inception to the End of the First Twelve Months.' Derbyshire: North Derbyshire Health Authority.

Kennedy, G. (2001) 'Intensive interaction.' *Learning Disability Practice 4*, 3, 14–17.

Knickerbocker, B. (1980) *A Holistic Approach to the Treatment of Learning Disorders.* Thorofare, NJ: Charles B. Slack, Inc.

Lin, S., Cermak, S., Coster, W. and Miller, L. (2005) 'The relationship between length of institutionalization and sensory integration in children adopted from eastern Europe.' *American Journal of Occupational Therapy 59*, 2, 139–147.

Longhorn, F. (1988) *A Sensory Curriculum for Very Special People. A Practical Approach to Curriculum Planning.* London: Souvenir Press.

REFERENCES

Marvin, C. (1998) 'Teaching and Learning for Children with Profound and Multiple Learning Difficulties.' In P. Lacey and C. Ouvrey, *People with Profound and Multiple Learning Disabilities: A Collaborative Approach to Meeting Complex Needs.* London: David Fulton.

Nind, M. and Hewett, D. (2001) *A Practical Guide to Intensive Interaction.* Kidderminster: British Institute of Learning Disabilities.

O'Brien, J. (1989) *What's Worth Working For? Leadership for Better Quality Human Services.* Lithonia, GA: Responsive Systems Associates.

O'Brien, J. and Lyle, C. (1987) *Framework for Accomplishment.* Lithonia, GA: Responsive Systems Associates.

Sanderson, H. (2000) 'Person Centred Planning: Key Features and Approaches', paper commissioned by the Joseph Rowntree Foundation.

Sanderson, H. and Gitsham, N. (1991) *A Holistic Sensory Approach: 'A Guide to Sensory Stimulation for People who have Profound Learning Disabilities'* (2nd edn). London: David Fulton.

Sanderson, H. and Harrison, J. with Price, S. (1996) *Aromatherapy and Massage for People with Learning Difficulties.* Leicestershire: Abbott Press Ltd.

Wilbarger, P. and Wilbarger, J. (1991) *Sensory Defensiveness in Children aged 2–12. An Intervention Guide for Parents and Other Caretakers.* Santa Barbara, CA: Avanti Educational Programs.

Further reading

Balandin, S. (2002) 'Message from the President.' *The ISAAC Bulletin 67*, 2.

Bozic, N. and Murdoch, H. (eds) (1996) *Learning Through Interaction, Technology and Children with Multiple Disabilities*. London: David Fulton.

Brudenell, P. (1986) *The other side of profound handicap*. London: Croom Helm.

Bunning, K. (1997) 'The Role of Sensory Reinforcements in Developing Interactions in Children with Learning Difficulties: A Collaborative Approach.' In M. Fawcus (ed.) (1997) *Children with Learning Difficulties: A Collaborative Approach to their Education*. London: Whurr.

Denziloe, J. (1994) *Fun and Games. Practical Leisure Ideas for People with Profound Disabilities*. Oxford: Butterworth-Heinemann Ltd.

Dunn, W., Brown, C. and McGuigan, A. (1994) 'The ecology of human performance: a framework for considering the effect of context.' *American Journal of Occupational Therapy 48*, 7, 595–607.

Grandin, T. (1995) *Thinking in Pictures*. New York: Doubleday.

Haylor, D. and Bradshaw, S. (ed. Flo Longhorn) (2005) *Feast of Music: Volumes 1 and 2*. Bedfordshire: Catalyst Education Resources Ltd.

Heller, S. (2002) *Too Loud, Too Bright, Too Fast, Too Tight. What to Do if You Are Sensory Defensive in an Overstimulating World*. New York: HarperCollins Publishers, Inc.

Hewett, D. and Nind, M. (eds) (1998) *Interaction in Action: Reflections on the Usse of Intensive Interaction*. London: David Fulton.

Hutchinson, R. and Kewin, J. (eds) (1994) *Sensations and Disability: Sensory Environments for Leisure, Snoezelen, Education and Therapy*. Chesterfield: ROMPA UK.

Kennedy, J., Sanderson, H. and Wilson, H. (2002) *Friendship and Community. Practical Strategies for Making Connections in Communities*. Manchester: North West Training and Development Team.

Longhorn, F. (1986) *The Other Side of Profound Handicap – 'A Practical Approach to Curriculum Planning.'* London: Souvenir Press.

Longhorn, F. (1993) *Planning a Multisensory Massage Programme for Very Special People*. Bedfordshire: Catalyst Education Resources Ltd.

Longhorn, F. (1993) *Prerequisites to Learning for Very Special People*. Bedfordshire: Catalyst Education Resources Ltd.

Longhorn, F. (1997) *Enhancing Education Through the Use of Ultraviolet Light and Fluorescing Materials*. Bedfordshire: Catalyst Education Resources Ltd.

Longhorn, F. (1997) *Sensory Cookery for Very Special People*. Bedfordshire: Catalyst Education Resources Ltd.

Longhorn, F. (2000) *Sensory Drama for Very Special People*. Bedfordshire: Catalyst Education Resources Ltd.

Longhorn, F. (2000) *Numeracy for Very Special People*. Bedfordshire: Catalyst Education Resources Ltd.

Longhorn, F. (2001) *Literacy for Very Special People*. Bedfordshire: Catalyst Education Resources Ltd.

Nind, M. and Hewett, D. (1994) *Access to Communication: Developing the Basics of Communication with People with Severe Learning Difficulties through Intensive Interaction*. London: David Fulton.